T0308002

The National Joker

THE NATIONAL JOKER

*Abraham Lincoln
and the Politics
of Satire*

TODD NATHAN THOMPSON

Southern Illinois University Press
Carbondale

Jacket illustration: detail from "May the Best Man Win—Uncle
Sam Reviewing the Army of Candidates for the Presidential
Chair." Thomas Nast, *Phunny Phellow*, April 1864, 8–9.
*Courtesy of The Rare Book and Manuscript Library of the
University of Illinois at Urbana-Champaign.*

Library of Congress Cataloging-in-Publication Data
Thompson, Todd Nathan.
The national joker : Abraham Lincoln and the politics of satire
/ Todd Nathan Thompson.
pages cm
Includes bibliographical references and index.
ISBN 978-0-8093-3422-3 (cloth : alk. paper)
ISBN 0-8093-3422-4 (cloth : alk. paper)
ISBN 978-0-8093-3423-0 (ebook)
ISBN 0-8093-3423-2 (ebook)
1. Lincoln, Abraham, 1809–1865—Humor. 2. Political satire,
American—History—19th century. 3. United States—Politics
and government—1861–1865—Humor. 4. Political culture—
United States—History—19th century. I. Title.
E457.15.T47 2015
973.7092—dc23   2014043670

*To Sara Stewart, who loved me even though
I was broken and convinced me that I
still had some chapters left to write*

Contents

List of Illustrations ix

Acknowledgments xi

Introduction: Abraham Lincoln and the American Satiric Tradition 1

CHAPTER 1
"This Reminds Me of a Little Joke": From Humor to Satire 9

CHAPTER 2
"Little Big Man": Modesty and Attack in Lincoln's Writings
and Speeches 41

CHAPTER 3
The Rail-Splitter President 64

CHAPTER 4
"Abraham Africanus the First": The Limits of
Preemptive Self-Satire 86

CHAPTER 5
"A Hoosier Michael Angelo": The Politics of Lincoln's Physical
Appearance in Popular Media 115

Notes 143

Bibliography 159

Index 173

Illustrations

"By the Way This Puts Me in the Mind of a Little Story" 13
"Great and Astonishing Trick of Old Abe, the Western Juggler" 26
"The National Joker" 27
"Columbia Demands Her Children!" 27
"I Knew Him, Horatio" 28
"This Reminds Me of a Little Joke" 32
Lincolniana, or Humors of Uncle Abe, cover 33
Old Abe's Joker, or Wit at the White House, cover 34
"The Tribune Offering the Chief Magistracy to the Western Cincinnatus" 75
"The Last Rail Split by 'Honest Old Abe'" 76
"'Uncle Sam' Making New Arrangements" 77
"Lincoln's Last Warning" 78
"Good Gracious, Abraham Lincoln!" 79
"The Rail Splitter at Work Repairing the Union" 80
"A Job for the New Cabinet Maker" 81
"Cooperation" 82
"Log Cabin Built by President Lincoln in Kentucky" 84
"President Lincoln's Inaugural" 87
"Masks and Faces" 91
"Lincoln Signing the Emancipation Proclamation" 91
"Abduction of the Yankee Goddess of Liberty" 92
The Lincoln Catechism, title page 94
Abraham Africanus I, title page 95

"First Black Republican Made in Old Kaintuck" 97
Untitled drawing, Richmond, Virginia 103
"The Great 'Cannon Game'" 107
"Pull Devil—Pull Baker" 110
"The Vampire" 111
"In for His Second Innings" 112
"Lincoln Out Walking" 117
"'Boy' Lost!" 126
"A Political Race" 127
"Lincoln, Douglas, and the Rail-Fence Handicap" 128
"May the Best Man Win" 129
"Presidential Cobblers and Wire-Pullers" 131
"The Good Uncle and the Naughty Boy" 132
"Long Abraham Lincoln a Little Longer" 134
"With All Thy Faults" 135
"Jeff Davis's November Nightmare" 136
"The Tallest Ruler on the Globe" 137
"A Phenomenon of Portraiture" 138

Illustrations

Acknowledgments

I am grateful to many people for their help in making this book happen. At the University of Illinois at Chicago, Robin Sandra Grey pushed my initial thinking on Lincoln and satire and encouraged me to pursue it in depth; Terence Whalen offered invaluable feedback and support as well. UIC also supported the project and provided time and money to research through a Dean's Scholar Award and Graduate College Provost's Research Award. I am also thankful to the staffs of the various libraries at which I conducted my research: the Library Company of Philadelphia, which kindly provided an Andrew W. Mellon Foundation Fellowship; the Lilly Library, which supported my research through an Everett Helm Visiting Fellowship; the Abraham Lincoln Presidential Library; and the American Antiquarian Society, where Ashley Cataldo was invaluable in helping me to collect many of the images in this book.

Sylvia Frank Rodrigue at Southern Illinois University Press has been indefatigable in her enthusiasm for the project from proposal to final draft and over the course of two years has helped to make this book much better. Wayne Larsen cheerfully and skillfully shepherded this project in its later stages. I am thankful to SIU Press's anonymous outside readers, whose comments and critiques were invaluable.

Megan O'Connor, Patricia O'Connor, Jessica Showalter, and Justin Tanaka also offered thoughtful and thorough readings of my work in its various stages. Mary Lou Kowaleski provided meticulous copyediting. My graduate assistants at Indiana University of Pennsylvania—Erin Guydish,

Shana Kraynak, Andru Lugo, and Kaitlin Tonti—were tireless in their efforts. Guydish, in particular, deserves praise for her two-year dedication to this project and her cheerful eagerness to embark on quixotic research quests and endless fact-checking. My colleagues at Indiana University of Pennsylvania, especially David Downing, Tony Farrington, Tanya Heflin, Gian Pagnucci, and Mike Sell, have been consistently supportive of my research. My graduate students, too, keep me hungry and remind me that I love to work.

I am most grateful to all my friends and family for sustaining me during the writing of this book. My mother, Joan Middleton, father, George Thompson, and brother, Cory Thompson, have long indulged my writerly sensibilities. I appreciate the diversion mandated over the past couple years by my friends, especially B. W. B. (aka Simeon Novels and Nate Wygonik), Sarah Slack, and Henry Wong Doe. Special thanks go to Garrett Brown, Madeleine Monson-Rosen, and Sara Stewart for their intellectual (and sometimes necessarily nonintellectual) companionship, for picking me up when I was down, and for patiently abiding my Lincoln jokes.

The National Joker

Introduction:
Abraham Lincoln
and the American
Satiric Tradition

Ihat Abraham Lincoln liked jokes—hearing them, telling them, drawing morals from them—was a truism in his time and has been much discussed by Lincoln scholars in ours. He read aloud pieces by humorists, such as Artemus Ward and Orpheus C. Kerr, to cabinet members (to Secretary of War Edwin M. Stanton's disgust), and cartoonist Frank Bellew dubbed him "the National Joker."[1] But political cartoons and print satires that mock Lincoln often traffic in precisely the same images and terms that Lincoln humorously used to characterize himself. Such convergence between popular depictions of Lincoln and Lincoln's own self-presentation is the subject of this book.

The National Joker: Abraham Lincoln and the Politics of Satire considers the politically productive dialectic between Abraham Lincoln's use of satire and satiric treatments of him in political cartoons, humor periodicals, joke books, and campaign literature. In his speeches, writings, and public persona, Lincoln combined modesty and attack, consistently engaging in strategic self-deprecation to deprecate his opponents, their policies, and their arguments, thus refiguring satiric discourse as political discourse (and vice versa). At the same time, he astutely deflected his opponents' criticisms of him by admitting, embracing, and, sometimes, preemptively initiating those criticisms. Lincoln also fostered an image ready-made for caricature—a fast-maturing political-cultural form when Lincoln first sought the presidency in 1860—and as such was able to mitigate partially the satiric content of cartoon portrayals as well as print portrayals of him. By self-fashioning himself as a folksy, fallible figure who lacked the prestige that caricature usually seeks to attack, Lincoln was able to use satire as a weapon without being severely wounded by it.[2]

Though much ink has been spilled in recounting Lincoln's famous sense of humor, few have labeled him a satirist. The relative paucity of scholarly attention to Lincoln's use of satire and of his treatments in the satires of his day may have something to do with the ways in which critics have categorized humor and satire over the past two centuries. A recent scholar of satire has convincingly shown that the nineteenth-century critical predilection to speak of American "humor" rather than "satire" was a result of lingering Anglophobia after the War of 1812. That is, Americans' "postwar triumphalism" led to a derogation, beginning in the 1810s, of the term "satire"—which to Americans at the time "connoted the worst of British culture"—in favor of "humor." Critics from the nineteenth century to today have, it seems, accepted this shift in terminology at face value and, thereby, characterized much American satire as humor.[3]

A brief survey of critical engagements with American humor and satire in popular nineteenth-century magazines underscores this point. For example, an 1867 essay on "Yankee Humor" in *Every Saturday: A Journal of Choice Reading* makes an odd distinction between humor and satire: the anonymous author praises James Russell Lowell's collection of anti–U.S.-Mexico War poems *The Biglow Papers* as "the most characteristic and complete expression of American humor" but then generalizes to announce, "[h]itherto slavery and politics have been the chief subjects of the best American humor. The great social satirist has to come."[4] Here political satire is recast as political *humor*, and satire is deferred as a genre that Americans have yet to master. A quick perusal of the titles of other retrospective accounts of late nineteenth-century humor and satire in the U.S. press reveals a tendency to characterize American humor in opposition to British satire. Articles such as Ellen A. Vinton's "Who Are Our American Humorists?" (1895), W. P. Trent's "A Retrospect of American Humor" (1901), and Joel Chandler Harris's "Humor in America" (1909) all concentrate on American works. On the other hand, articles with "satire" in the title tend to discuss British authors: examples include "English Satire" (1863), which mentions no Americans, and "Political Satire and Satirists" (1842), which only describes in passing a few Revolutionary-era satirists, such as Joel Barlow and Philip Freneau.[5] That even a nationalist, Young America organ like *The United States Magazine and Democratic Review* (edited by John. L. O'Sullivan, who coined the term "manifest destiny"), which published "Political Satire and Satirists," would slight Americans in its discussions of satire shows just how associated with Englishness the term had become by midcentury. Similarly, James Hannay's *Satire and Satirists* (1855), a series of lectures collected in book form, begins with Horace and Juvenal, proceeds through early European and neoclassical British satire, and ends with mostly British writers (discussing, among others, Lord George Gordon Byron, Tom Moore, and Theodore Hook) and no Americans in his chapter on the "Present Aspect of Satirical Literature."[6]

Such classifications spring from U.S. authors' and critics' desire to situate humor as a key element of "Americanness," a penchant that Lincoln scholars have followed in describing Lincoln's humor as the epitome of a particular national trait. Harris, for example, argues for a peculiarly American sense of humor that characterizes its political, social, and religious institutions: "It may be said of us, with some degree of truth, that we have a way of living humorously, and are conscious of the fact; that our view of life and its responsibilities is, to say the least, droll and comfortable; and there seems never to have been a day in our history when the American view of things generally was not charged or trimmed with humor." Harris highlights the centrality (and efficacy) of the comic in American political campaigns and credits Lincoln's droll sense of humor for his political success: "American diplomacy has achieved its greatest victories since the chair of state has been occupied by a gentleman who was noted for his humor long before his statesmanship had been put to the test."[7] In connecting Lincoln's penchant for humor with "victories" of "diplomacy," Harris by insinuation further undermines distinctions between humor and satire that his essay's title purports to invoke.

Because Lincoln told nonpolitical jokes in political situations and shared private anecdotes that subsequently circulated widely in the public sphere, differentiating humor from satire and public from private can be somewhat dizzying if we define satire as an aesthetic attack mounted in a humorous or playful tone through literary indirection (e.g., metaphor or allegory or hyperbole) against a public figure, policy, or idea.[8] Lincoln deployed his apolitical stories allegorically to describe situations that were precisely political, shifting these jokes from the realm of humor to that of satire. In short, Lincoln, time and time again throughout his political career, repurposed jokes for political ends, in the process transmuting humor into satire.

Abraham Lincoln, Satirist-Statesman Satirized

Lincoln may be viewed as the culmination of an American tradition of "satirist-statesmen," politically powerful figures who addressed pressing issues via two channels simultaneously: that of direct, political arguments or official diplomacy and that of indirect, aesthetic engagement through satire voiced by characters, personae, or self-presentations with ties to the people. Like satirist-statesmen before him, such as Benjamin Franklin, who as "Homespun" pilloried the Stamp Act in letters to the British press before testifying against the act before the House of Commons, or Hugh Henry Brackenridge, who satirized the western Pennsylvania Whiskey Rebellion after trying to mediate it, or fellow Whig congressman David Crockett, who leveraged his "half man, half alligator" image into national celebrity as a rustic foil against which to measure and mock Jacksonian Democrats, Lincoln used satire for political ends, simultaneously ingratiating himself with constituents as a common man and attacking or belittling his opponents and their policies as out of touch.[9] As writers and speakers, all of these politicians donned satiric or self-satiric masks to launch attacks from selective positions of powerlessness, speaking in humbler, less official, and cruder voices meant to approximate those of political outsiders more than those of their political peers. In satires featuring homey characters, personae, or self-presentations, satirist-statesmen encouraged their readers to identify with them and against their defamiliarized targets, who were often portrayed as personifications of official, entrenched, or authoritarian power. This very awareness of and facility with satire helped Lincoln to deflect preemptively, or at least minimize, the sting of political satires levied against him. That the central figure in American history was also its ultimate satirist-statesman, whose satiric discourse was his political discourse, speaks to the heretofore unexamined prevalence and power of political satire in nineteenth-century America.

Lincoln's legendarily self-deprecating performances of modesty were key to his satire (and to other early and antebellum satirist-statesmen's). Other scholars have limned a tradition of modest satire, which features humble, "plain, common-sense" characters who act as rustic "counsels of prudence" through "horse sense" and folk wisdom. But the "horse-sense character and the fool character, who were to be stand-bys for humorists for a long time," often were embodied in the same persona.[10] Lincoln, for one, following in this line of humorous rustics, situated himself as comically fallible but, nonetheless, wise.

4

This inclusion of the satirist as among the targets of his or her own laughter is integral to the efficacy of modest satire in its expression of what one satire critic has labeled the "satirist-satirized," which arises when "the satirist becomes self-conscious about his [or her] own activity." That is, when the satirist realizes how problematic is his or her "own place as a judging and observing subject, he [or she] begins to reckon himself [or herself] into the universal condemnation which only awaited his [or her] own presence to be complete."[11] The satirist's inclusion of him- or herself as a target is a necessary ingredient of any broader societal critique. Of course, the danger of "universal condemnation" is that assailing *everything* risks conservatism and inactivity, for there is no particular change that such a satire's readership could undertake or even conceive; "universal condemnation," thus, paradoxically treats political critiques as of merely literary concern.[12] Lincoln was "self-conscious about his own activity" but aimed at more specific targets than "universal condemnation"; his satiric sallies were modest and self-conscious but precisely aimed.

For literary critic Kenneth Burke, "true irony" does not claim superiority over the target it seeks to represent through reduction. Just as important, the satirist satirized's self-awareness also allows for the "imagination" of alternatives or "some measure of development beyond folly" that counters the paralysis of totalizing critique.[13] Such emphasis on the satirist's intentionality in articulating self-satire runs counter to poststructuralist-inspired claims that satirists lose control of their irony and accidentally permit their attacks either to boomerang back upon them or to expand outward infinitely into "universal condemnation." Rather, Lincoln—as nineteenth-century America's consummate satirist-statesman satirized—engaged in self-satire strategically to sanction his critiques of other figures as well as to mitigate others' denunciations of him.

Elsewhere, Burke muses, "If I am to write a satire, when all the returns are in it mustn't turn out that I am holier than thou. I must be among my victims."[14] This self-awareness of his own complicity in the situation he hopes to satirize grounds his satiric critique and defends him from charges of hypocrisy. Such inclusion of oneself in one's satiric reproof disarms the audience and sanctions the critique as thorough and honest. For example, when in an 1848 speech Lincoln, serving his only term in the U.S. House of Representatives, mocked his own war record (as a captain in the Black Hawk War) and then attacked that of Senator Lewis Cass (Democratic presidential candidate and War of 1812 hero), Lincoln's prefatory self-satire

displayed to his audience his self-effacing good humor and preempted coun-
terattacks on him, as he had already occupied that ground himself. Much
of Lincoln's satire of others begins in self-satire; if he is attacking anyone,
it seems, it is himself. But these self-directed attacks almost always either
sought larger game—secondary targets who were subsequently demeaned
by comparison—or else inoculated Lincoln against similar criticisms by
his opponents, thus defusing their attacks on him while presenting himself
as genial. Lincoln's good humor also derived, in part, from his consciously
performed rusticity. In repurposing jokes or stories, most people will adapt
their language and referents to fit the level of sophistication of their varying
audiences, but Lincoln did not do this. In his Kentucky, Indiana, and early
Illinois days, Lincoln swapped his stories with rugged western folk; when he
turned politician and resorted to his humorous anecdotes in front of more
sophisticated auditors in Springfield, Chicago, and Washington, he rarely
changed his style, he kept his western accent, and he sometimes played
to stereotypes that easterners had of him as a frontier rustic. Though the
Democratic *Chicago Times* may have complained of the difficulty in rendering Lincoln's speeches "in intelligible English" for print, P. M. Zall, who has
collected myriad Lincoln jokes and witticisms, points out, "To many readers
that was exactly the way he was supposed to talk. He sounded just like the
westerners they knew from stories in their newspapers and magazines."
Such performance required not only a genuine common touch but also
sophisticated media savvy. Like the southwestern humorists who were his
contemporaries, he was able to stand both inside and outside of small-town
western life, to laugh at it while being part of it. Lincoln was, thus, in one
sense, akin to a "crackerbox philosopher," a classic American comic figure
who, according to one scholar, is "a symbol of a class-conscious people, a
personification of the folk" and through "wise saws and rustic anecdotes
and deliberately cruel innuendo . . . interprets the provincial eccentricities
of American life and the petty corruptions of American political intrigue."[15]
Lincoln consciously performed this tradition while co-opting its humor
for political ends.

Lincoln, thus, spoke satirically in multiple registers simultaneously.
In satire, more than in any other mode or genre, the (sometimes multiple)
masks that a satirist dons create a dialogue not only between different
vocabularies and characters in the text but also between the satirist and
his or her speaker(s), as well as between satiric representations and their
real-world referents. Such layered dialogues collide "official" and "unofficial"

languages in complicated interrelationships of ridicule and self-ridicule.[16] Lincoln, for instance, famously told comic stories in the unpretentious idiom "of the farm and frontier," but he could also, as one critic puts it, "speak and write in the most beautiful, clear, and direct prose ever known to American politics." Helen Nicolay went so far as to say, "Lincoln knew no foreign tongue, yet he spoke two languages—the vernacular, and a strong, majestic prose, akin to poetry." Such verbal dialogism allowed Lincoln to engage in satiric leveling, demeaning his opponents to his own, artificially diminished level. At the same time, attempts to use satiric leveling against Lincoln often fell flat simply because Lincoln had already modestly demeaned himself in terms not too different from those used by his attackers.[17]

Hence, as *The National Joker* argues, Lincoln was adept not only at using satire but also at deflecting it. Lincoln time and time again turned negative assumptions or depictions of him—as ugly, cowardly, jocular, inexperienced—into positive traits of the "self-made man" while demeaning the traditionally positively charged political symbols of heroism, greatness, and prestige. He defined himself against such traits through his humorous manner, his tousled physical presentation, his self-deprecating modesty, and his (often sarcastic) deference. Mapping these qualities to the affective power of the American Dream, Lincoln in his political self-fashioning shifted his humor to a sign of shrewdness and compassion, his awkward lankiness to a metaphor for his stature as a leader, his modesty to greatness, and his laboring past to a symbol for his political pragmatism.

As a politician, Lincoln used these same strategies of redefinition and deflection to shape a symbolic self presented to the populace; his "public image" was, thus, defined by his versions of others' characterizations of him. In the American context, self-fashioning is inextricably linked to the reigning American myth of the self-made man. Lincoln used modest self-satire—and an embrace of others' satires of him—to highlight the very fact of his self-making by foregrounding both his current position and his humble origins. Even southerners like Harris came to praise Lincoln's humor as "essentially the humor of the common people, the people who have made the Republic what it is, and who will continue to mold its destiny," demonstrating the power of Lincoln's symbiotic performances of humor and of the self-made man.[18] Through performed modesty, folksy stories, and self-satirizing raillery of himself and his political opponents, Lincoln exerted some control over his own image while assailing those of his enemies. The symbiotic relationship of Lincoln's satiric self-fashioning, his satiric attacks on other politicians, and satiric treatments of him is the subject of the chapters of *The National Joker* that follow.

Of course, the sheer volume of scholarship on Lincoln is already intimidatingly immense, and in forwarding this new intervention into Lincoln studies, I stand atop many broad and prominent shoulders. Scholars like Benjamin P. Thomas, Robert Bray, and Zall have laid important groundwork for this study in their characterizations of Lincoln's comic sensibility.[19] Several biographies of Lincoln have also noted the centrality of the comic to Lincoln's thinking and writing and his use of satire for political ends.[20] Historians, such as Harold Holzer, Gary L. Bunker, Gabor S. Boritt, Mark E. Neely, and Robert S. Harper, have carefully studied representations of Lincoln in the popular press.[21] But none of these scholars considers precisely *how* Lincoln took advantage of political cartoons and other media to help proliferate a particular Lincoln image—studiously built by self-fashioning and self-presentation—through, not in spite of, satires and caricatures of him. And none considers the reciprocal relationship between Lincoln's use *of* satire to his treatment *in* satires. This is the project of *The National Joker*.

CHAPTER 1

"This Reminds Me
of a Little Joke":
From Humor to Satire

You speak of Lincoln stories. I don't think that is a correct
phrase. I don't make the stories mine by telling them. I am
only a retail dealer.

—Abraham Lincoln to Noah Brooks

An estimated 60 percent of the stories assigned to Lincoln in his lifetime
can be traced to previously printed sources, such as humorists like Joseph
Glover Baldwin, Artemus Ward, Petroleum V. Nasby, and Charles Halpine;
old joke books like *Joe Miller's Jest Book*; and tidbits from newspaper columns
or periodicals like *Harper's Monthly*.[1] Contrary to his claim to Noah Brooks,
though, Lincoln did in a sense "make the stories" his when he retold them,
for in applying generalized jests to specific political situations, he transmuted
these jokes, anecdotes, and fables from humor to satire. Throughout his
career, Lincoln put his most common source materials—namely, Aesop's
fables, jokes circulating in the popular press, southwestern humorists, and,
later, northern dialect humorists—to satirical use. In a reciprocal relationship with the popular press, Lincoln not only gleaned source material for
his satire but also saw his stories—real and imagined—circulated widely,
thereby recursively augmenting his reputation as the "National Joker."

Lincoln and his compatriots certainly viewed the stories and jokes he
repurposed as political and satiric. In *Frank Leslie's Illustrated Newspaper*

in 1863, Secretary of State William H. Seward, for example, praised the practical usefulness of Lincoln's stories: "Mr. Lincoln never tells a joke for a joke's sake, they are like the parables of old—lessons of wisdom." And after Lincoln's death, eulogists came to appreciate Lincoln's method of thinking and arguing through comic narratives, though many had disparaged the habit from the outset of his presidency. Ralph Waldo Emerson, for example, celebrated Lincoln's ability to utter thoughts "so disguised as pleasantries that it is certain they had no reputation at first but as jests; and only later, by the very acceptance and adoption they find in the mouths of millions, turn out to be the wisdom of the hour." *New York Times* editor Henry J. Raymond, who wrote an 1865 biography of the president, *Life and Public Services of Abraham Lincoln*, concurred: "Much has been said of Mr. Lincoln's habit of telling stories, and it could scarcely be exaggerated. He had a keen sense of the humorous and the ludicrous, and relished jokes and anecdotes for the amusement they afforded him. But story-telling was with him rather a mode of stating and illustrating facts and opinions, than anything else. . . . Mr. Lincoln often gave clearness and force to his ideas by pertinent anecdotes and illustrations drawn from daily life." Even Lincoln himself pointed to the political advantages of his anecdotes. Silas W. Burt recalled Lincoln as saying, "It is not the story itself, but its purpose, or effect, that interests me." Railroad president and New York Republican leader Chauncey M. Depew remembered Lincoln telling him, "in reference to some sharp criticisms which had been made upon his storytelling . . . 'I have found in the course of a long experience that common people'—and repeating it '—common people, take them as they run, are more easily influenced and informed through the medium of a broad illustration than in any other way, and as to what the hypercritical few may think, I don't care.'" A key word here is "informed," revealing as it does Lincoln's view of satiric stories as political education for nonspecialists. As Nathaniel Grigsby told Lincoln's law partner William H. Herndon in an 1865 interview, "Mr Lincoln was figurative in his Speeches—talks & conversations. He argued much from Analogy and Explained things hard for us to understand by stories—maxims—tales and figures. He would almost always point his lesson or idea by some story that was plain and near as that we might instantly see the force & bearing of what he said." In this way, Lincoln's use of figurative language served as political education—or, as one Lincoln scholar describes it, "the gradual *education* of public opinion."[2] Lincoln's

"This Reminds Me of a Little Joke"

justification for his storytelling and his contemporaries' assessments of it highlight its political goals: to convince and instruct through indirect illustration or to gently reprove others' actions, all while molding a homey public image.

Formally, jokes, on the one hand, usually operate through delineations of general, recognizable types or stereotypes (e.g., the country minister, the rube, the racialized stereotype, the Yankee sharper, etc.). Satire, on the other hand, identifies and attacks a much more specific satiric referent, usually a particular public person or policy. Lincoln's retelling of jokes, fables, and humorous anecdotes in political settings worked by replacing general types with specific referents, or he let his audience make these replacements, which allowed him to remain genial, seemingly above the fray of public attack by speaking indirectly and allegorically. Such indirection is key to satire, which "proceeds by methods which are manifestly not those of direct, literal communication (and thus involves what has been variously described as obliquity, indirection, irony, invention, distortion, etc., etc.)."[3] At the same time, telling these anecdotes displayed the common touch that ingratiated him with constituents.

Just as important, in using a story, joke, or parable to describe a specific situation or moment, Lincoln, in effect, redefined that situation or moment in his own terms, which gave him a distinct polemical advantage. All satires engage in a referential act, though *the degree and kind of referentiality* differ from one satire to the next. The historical particulars to which a satire refers are "neither wholly fact nor wholly fiction." That is, in creating a satire, the satirist also constructs his or her own, alternate version of events, thus displacing or competing with another's history. As one satire theorist explains, "To assume that a satirist *or* a historian is simply referring to 'truth' or 'history,'" then, "is to be persuaded by that writer's version of events."[4] When Lincoln used an illustrative joke or story to talk about politics, he changed not only the story through reapplication but also the situation it had been leveraged to describe. Or, to speak in terms of metaphor, he slyly shifted both vehicle and tenor. When Lincoln's auditors acquiesced to the logic of his joke and when they recognized its metaphorical application, they were in a sense agreeing to his definitions of the situation under discussion. They, thus, came, usually unconsciously, to accept his version of history. This is how "Lincoln stories" moved out of the realm of recycled humor of folksy anecdotes and into the realm of polemical satire.

"Aesop of the New World": The Politics of
Lincoln's Jokes and Fables

Biographers and historians who trace Lincoln's early literary influences emphasize his love of Shakespeare, Robert Burns, and Aesop's fables. Several authors connect Lincoln's facility as a communicator to the figurative language that permeates his favorite books (i.e., the King James Bible, fables, Shakespeare's plays, and *Pilgrim's Progress*). Lincoln drew from his favorite sources not just metaphorical indirectness but also comic language and timing. He loved Burns's "satiric sharpness, his identification with the common man" and drew from Burns's poem "Tam O'Shanter," which Lincoln had memorized and often recited aloud in his storytelling.[5] Among other things, Burns taught Lincoln to use dialect comically but without coming off as pandering or insulting to the common people he lovingly mimicked.

If Burns greatly influenced the style of Lincoln's storytelling, Aesop's fables provided him with a wealth of source material. These fables were one of Lincoln's "lifelong delights" and the likely reason for his penchant for "explication by anecdote." Lincoln consistently applied the lessons of allegory and "moral analogy," which he had learned and cherished from Aesop's fables, for political purposes.[6] The press recognized this connection, and in 1863 *Frank Leslie's Illustrated Newspaper* dubbed the president "the Aesop of the new world." Similarly, the 1863 illustrated pamphlet *Ye Book of Copperheads* features an image of Lincoln as a file, which a sympathizer to the Southern cause (pictured as a snake coiled around the file) attempts unsuccessfully to bite (fig. 1.1). Lincoln says, "By the way this puts me in mind of a little Story in Esop's Fables."[7] The image itself refers to the Aesop fable "The Serpent and the File," in which a serpent tries to sink its fangs into a file that pricks the snake's skin, but, of course, the snake can do no harm to the insensible object. This image, thus, associates Lincoln's love for stories with both wisdom and toughness.

Lincoln's reputation as an allegorist is apparently well founded, as he leveraged fables to simplify or redefine complex situations before and during the Civil War. For example, Lincoln's old friend Joshua Speed recalled Lincoln adapting one of Aesop's fables in his reply to William Cabell Rives, who when serving on a Washington commission seeking to avoid the Civil War, apparently urged Lincoln to surrender federal property, including forts, in the South. According to Speed,

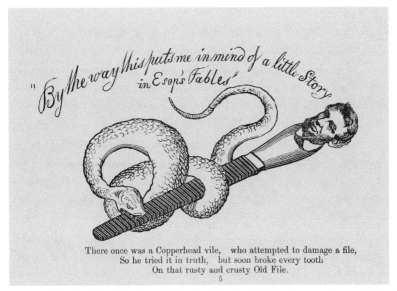

There once was a Copperhead vile, who attempted to damage a file,
So he tried it in truth, but soon broke every tooth
On that rusty and crusty Old File.
5

Figure 1.1. "By the Way This Puts Me in the Mind of a Little Story in Esop's Fables."
Ye Book of Copperheads *(Philadelphia: Leypoldt, 1863): 5. Courtesy, American Antiquarian Society.*

Mr. Lincoln asked him if he remembered the fable of the Lion and the Woodsman's daughter. Mr. Reeves [*sic*] said that he did not. Aesop, said the President, reports that a lion was very much in love with a woodsman's daughter. The fair maid, afraid to say no, referred him to her father. The lion applied for the girl. The father replied, your teeth are too long. The lion went to a dentist and had them extracted. Returning, he asked for his bride. No, the woodsman said, your claws are too long. Going back to the dentist, he had them drawn. Then, returning to claim his bride, the woodsman, seeing that he was disarmed, beat out his brains. "May it not be so," Mr. Lincoln said, "with me, if I give up all that is asked."

Zall notes that the story as Lincoln tells it differs from the contemporary translation of Aesop by Thomas James, wherein the woodsman merely drives away "the unreasonable suitor."[8] Lincoln's revision here makes the story more ominous and, therefore, a better fit to the martial decisions of the time. But the fable operates like a joke, in that it personifies abstract complexities into recognizable character types (the woodsman, the kind daughter, the lion), allowing Lincoln to explain his perspective from a new point of view on surrendering federal property in the South.

Jesus also taught through parables, and the Bible provided Lincoln with another trove of images and stories that he could use to make political points. Because nineteenth-century Americans were, in general, extremely literate in biblical language and narratives, biblical allusions operated as a kind of lingua franca. Lincoln took considerable advantage of this fact. For instance, in accepting the Republican nomination to run against Stephen A. Douglas for a seat in the U.S. Senate, Lincoln in his House Divided speech on June 16, 1858, quoted Ecclesiastes 9:4 to excoriate Douglas for the Kansas-Nebraska Act. Lincoln, speaking of Douglas and the act, told the crowd, "They remind us that *he* is a very *great man*, and that the largest of *us* are very small ones. Let this be granted. But 'a *living dog* is better than a *dead lion*.' Judge Douglas, if not a *dead* lion *for this work*, is at least a *caged* and *toothless* one."[9] Lincoln was responding, in part, to rumors that Douglas might garner Republican support for his reelection bid, in which case Lincoln would no doubt be asked to step aside.[10] In aiming Ecclesiastes 9:4 squarely at Douglas and his tarnished reputation, Lincoln made the passage satiric by giving it a specific referent. In doing so, he leveraged his crowd's moral assumptions for use against his satiric target and political rival. Democrats, in turn, during the 1858 campaign used Lincoln's own metaphor against him, describing him as a "puppy-dog fighting a lion."[11]

Secular sources of wit abounded in nineteenth-century America as well, and Lincoln also mined comic almanacs, joke books, and newspapers for humor that he could apply to his political life. J. H. Cheney tells of seeking Lincoln on a legal matter in spring 1859 and finding him "in the office reading what I took to be a comic almanac. He seemed to be very much amused and would frequently chuckle to himself." The George Philip Hambrecht manuscripts at the Lilly Library, Indiana University, in listing Lincoln's books, offer multiple entries of the well-known *Joe Miller's Jests* and the *American Almanac*; Robert Bray's annotated list of Lincoln's books also includes the eighteenth-century joke books *Joe Miller's Jests* and *Quin's Jests*.[12]

In fact, many Lincoln stories are actually old Joe Miller jokes repurposed for modern events. For example, Admiral John Dahlgren—who was in charge of the Washington Navy Yard and spoke often with Lincoln—recorded in his diary Lincoln's use of a very old joke, which in the 1845 edition of *Joe Miller's Jests* had been about King George III and General James Wolfe, who won fame for taking Quebec in the Seven Years' War. In 1862 Lincoln used the joke to describe his old political enemy James Shields, who, now a general, had fought off Stonewall Jackson at the Shenandoah Valley. Dahlgren

"This Reminds Me of a Little Joke"

writes, "About five o'clock A.M. the President came in from his room half dressed, and sat down between the Secretary [Stanton] and myself. He was reminded of a joke, at which we laughed heartily." In the next day's entry, Dahlgreen elaborates, "The President remarked yesterday that Shields was said to be crazy, which put him in mind that George III had been told the same of one of his generals, viz., that he was mad. The king replied he wished he would bite his other generals." Here Lincoln kept the context of the original joke—that is, King George and the Seven Years' War—but clearly offered an analogy to Shields by remarking that he was "said to be crazy." The satiric target of this joke was not Shields, nor even necessarily "other generals," but, rather, military standards and propriety that had little to do with actual fighting. Lincoln retold this joke in an interview a year later with updated referents: he replaced King George with himself, changed Wolfe to Ulysses S. Grant, and switched whiskey for madness.[13] This shows just how adaptable such jokes were for Lincoln.

A similar adaptability is at work in an old joke that Lincoln seems to have told for different purposes at different times. A version of the joke had been in circulation since the seventeenth century, but Lincoln probably knew it from Seba Smith's update of it in his Jack Downing letter "My First Visit to Portland," initially published in 1830 and reprinted in 1858 in W. S. Burton's *Cyclopedia of Wit and Humor*. According to Reverend George Minier, who had known Lincoln when he was a circuit lawyer, he told the joke to express bafflement at tariffs.

> [T]here is something obscure about it. It reminds me of the fellow that came into a grocery down here in Menard County, at Salem, where I once lived, and called for a picayune's worth of crackers; so the clerk laid them out on the counter. After sitting awhile, he said to the clerk, "I don't want these crackers, take them, and give me a glass of cider." So the clerk put the crackers back into the box, and handed the fellow the cider. After drinking, he started for the door. "Here, Bill," called out the clerk, "pay me for your cider." "Why," said Bill, "I gave you the crackers for it." "Well, then, pay me for the crackers." "But I haint had any;" responded Bill. "That's so," said the clerk. "Well, clear out! It seems to me that I've lost a picayune somehow, but I can't make it out exactly." "So," said Lincoln, after the laugh had subsided, "it is with the tariff; somebody gets the picayune, but I don't exactly understand how."

Obviously, there is nothing inherently political about this joke, which basically plays out a verbal shell game. The tariff issue is only brought in at the beginning and the end, as a contextualizing frame. By presenting himself as the confused clerk, Lincoln put himself in the politically awkward position of denying pretensions to technical knowledge on the subject. The implied argument is not that the tariff is necessarily bad for the country but that it is confusing and *feels* like fraud. In this way Lincoln—always a supporter of Whig policies of protective tariffs as encouraging industrial growth—aimed at collegiality with his audience, whom he expected to be confused by and suspicious of the tariff. Since it is only the frame and the idea of bafflement that makes the joke germane to the tariff issue in the first place, it is not surprising that Lincoln used the same joke in other political circumstances. For instance, when he told it in 1856, it was set in a restaurant, crackers became ginger cake, and Douglas's plan of popular sovereignty was substituted for the tariff. Chicago lawyer John J. McGilvra recalled hearing Lincoln tell the same story at a White House gathering in response to a guest's Kentucky story during the winter of 1863–64.[14]

Of course, Lincoln was not the only person in mid-nineteenth-century America recirculating old jokes. Newspapers and magazines also spread and popularized humor, and Lincoln, an avid consumer of popular media, was not averse to repurposing newspaper and magazine wit for political speech. When, for instance, he used the language of a tall tale in his sixth debate with Douglas on October 13, 1858, to describe Douglas's evolving principle of popular sovereignty as "thin as the homoepathic soup that was made by boiling the shadow of a pigeon that had starved to death [*Roars of laughter and cheering*]," he was recycling an image from *Harper's Monthly*.[15] If his auditors recognized it, they could feel a sense of commiseration with the candidate as a fellow devourer of printed media. If they did not, he came off as an original humorist.

Sometimes, Lincoln did not even have to tell a whole joke to get an audience response, so confident was he of his auditors' familiarity with circulating humor. In his seventh and final debate with Douglas on October 15, 1858, Lincoln mocked Douglas's ongoing fight with the James Buchanan administration. In fall 1857, proslavery Kansans dominated the Lecompton constitutional convention—mostly because Free Soilers had considered delegate elections fraudulent and boycotted the vote—and submitted a proslavery constitution to Congress. Buchanan, in a December 8 special message to Congress, urged admission of Kanas as a state despite

"This Reminds Me of a Little Joke"

its unrepresentative constitution. Douglas, concerned that the Lecompton constitution would hurt his reelection chances, denounced the president's message then and had been at loggerheads with him ever since.[16] Lincoln complimented Douglas for being "more severe upon the Administration than I had heard him upon any former occasion." He wanted Douglas to "give it to them with all the power he had" but also admitted that he "would be very much obliged if they would *Give it to him* in about the same way." Summarizing his feelings on the subject, Lincoln told the crowd, "All I can say now is to recommend to him and to them what I then commended—to prosecute the war against one another in the most vigorous manner. I say to them again—'Go it, husband!—Go it, bear!' [*Great laughter.*]"[17] Here Lincoln offers only the punch line to a well-known joke about a frontier woman who cannot decide whom she wants to win a fight between her rough-and-tumble husband and a bear. His setup mirrors the joke's but does not allude to it at all; Lincoln trusted his audience's comic literacy and felt that he need not point to the allegorical comparison he was making. The punch line is also funny in its rendering of Lincoln and Douglas as a married couple, given the increasing animosity of the debates.

Other examples of Lincoln repurposing newspaper and magazine quips are myriad. For instance, in illustrating "a fair sample of the way some people always do business," Lincoln retold a popular story from *Harper's Weekly* about a cooper who accidentally enclosed his son in a barrel after asking him to get inside and hold up the top as he finished assembling it. Lincoln also offered an anecdote—which had appeared in *Frank Leslie's Illustrated Newspaper* in 1856—about pigs crawling through fence rails so crooked that "every time the hogs got out they found themselves back in the same pasture again"—in order to prove "the absurdity of an army plan that would follow the Yazoo River to come at the Mississippi."[18] In these cases and others, Lincoln made humorous, politically neutral magazine anecdotes function satirically to redescribe political or military situations.

Lincoln, Partisan Politics, and Southwestern Humor

Even more influential to Lincoln's political style than timeless jokes was the tradition of southwestern humor, which flourished exactly during the span of Lincoln's political career, the 1830s into the 1860s. He owned Joseph Glover Baldwin's famous *Flush Times in Alabama and Mississippi* (1853) and reportedly told Baldwin that he kept a copy under his pillow.[19] As with the jokes and fables that he leveraged for political ends, Lincoln often retold scenes from *Flush Times* and other works of southwestern humor and in doing so once again transformed humor into satire. For example, an 1867 *Harper's Magazine* notes Lincoln's recourse to a scene from *Flush Times* in response to a petitioner asking him to release men, women, and children detained by General David Hunter, famous for his unauthorized 1862 order, which Lincoln quickly rescinded, to free slaves in Georgia, South Carolina, and Florida. In Lincoln's version of the story, a judge who was fond of handing out fines blamed all present in his courtroom when a stove pipe fell and interrupted court business. He yelled to his clerk to "enter a fine against every one in the room, women and children excepted." Though the petitioner was, doubtless, not amused at being put off by such a story, in telling it Lincoln deflected the petitioner's implied criticism while expressing his understanding of the issues involved. Lincoln's recourse to Baldwin's humor is also evident in an 1865 recollection by painter Francis Carpenter, who resided at the White House for six months while completing a portrait of Lincoln. Carpenter recounted a *Flush Times* scene Lincoln told about Baldwin's character Sar Kasem.[20]

Lincoln's use of southwestern humor as a political-satirical tactic extends far back, to as early as 1832, when, according to J. Rowan Herndon, a New Salem settler and cousin of William Herndon, Lincoln gave a political speech in which he told a story about a "meeting-house" that

> was in the woods and quite a distance from any other house. It was only used once a month. The preacher—an old line Baptist—was dressed in coarse linen pantaloons, and shirt of the same material. The pants, manufactured after the old fashion, with baggy legs and a flap in front, were made to attach to his frame without the aid of suspenders. A single button held his shirt in position, and that was at the collar. He rose up in the pulpit and with a loud voice announced his text thus: "I am the Christ, whom I shall represent to-day." About this time a little blue lizard ran up underneath his roomy pantaloons. The old preacher, not wishing to interrupt the steady flow of his sermon, slapped away on his legs, expecting to arrest the intruder; but his efforts were unavailing, and the little fellow kept on ascending higher and higher. Continuing the sermon, the preacher slyly loosened the central button which graced the waist-band of his pantaloons and with a kick off came that easy-fitting garment. But meanwhile Mr. Lizard had passed the equatorial line of waist-band and was calmly

"This Reminds Me of a Little Joke"

exploring that part of the preacher's anatomy which lay underneath the back of his shirt. Things were now growing interesting, but the sermon was still grinding on. The next movement on the preacher's part was for the collar button, and with one sweep of his arm off came the tow linen shirt. The congregation sat for an instant as if dazed; at length one old lady in the rear of the room rose up and glancing at the excited object in the pulpit, shouted at the top of her voice, "If you represent Christ then I'm done with the Bible."

This story comes straight from "Parson John Bullen's Lizards," a sketch of Sut Lovingood, the pseudonym of George Washington Harris, which recounts the above scene as a retributive practical joke on an overzealous preacher. The sketch appeared in Sut Lovingood's 1867 book *Sut Lovingood: Yarns Spun by a Nat'ral Born Durn'd Fool*. This could mean that Herndon misremembered Lincoln's 1832 anecdote and unwittingly replaced it with Lovingood's or, more likely, that versions of the story had been in circulation for over thirty years; Harris's sketch certainly fits within a long tradition of camp-meeting tales. But most important here is Herndon's description of the purpose of the anecdote, which he said Lincoln "told somewhere in his speech, in reply to some of the opposite candidates, who had represented themselves something extra."[21] Most scholars of southwestern humor see it as politically motivated but not necessarily satire. But Lincoln, in recontextualizing the comic story as a parable for politicians who "represented themselves something extra," once again changed the joke's referent from a general type (country preacher, rubes) to particular candidates who could be described and, thus, satirically leveled by comparison to that general type. It is in this way that Lincoln made southwestern humor function as political satire.

Lincoln had much in common with prominent southwestern humorists. First of all, many southwestern humorists were, like Lincoln, lawyers who swapped stories in small-town courthouses and taverns while riding the circuit. Baldwin was both a lawyer and a politician; Augustus Longstreet, author of the seminal work of southwestern humor, *Georgia Scenes*, was a circuit-riding lawyer; humorists Johnson Hooper (pseudonym Simon Suggs) and Solomon Franklin Smith also worked as lawyers. Contemporaries and modern critics alike have noted the influence of the profession's tradition of oral storytelling on southwestern humor. Philip Paxton, in *A Stray Yankee in Texas* (1853), for instance, contends that circuit court lawyers, living as they do in the thinly inhabited portion of our land, and among a class of persons generally very far their inferiors in point of education, rarely enjoying anything that may deserve the name of intellectual society, are too apt to seek for amusement in listening to the droll stories and odd things always to be heard at the country store or bar-room. Every new expression and queer tale is treasured up, and new ones manufactured against the happy time when they shall meet their *brothers-in-law* at the approaching term of the district court.

If ever pure fun, broad humor, and "Laughter holding both his sides," reign supreme, it is during the evening of these sessions. Each one empties and distributes his well filled budget of wit and oddities, receiving ample payment in like coin, which he pouches, to again disseminate at his earliest opportunity.[22]

Paxton's description evinces not only the scenes of camaraderie in which Lincoln and his fellows, like several southwestern humorists and theirs, swapped stories and honed their satiric styles but also the ways in which comic stories could circulate at regular intervals through the rural court circuit.

In addition to sharing a profession, most southwestern humorists were, like Lincoln, political Whigs, a fact that has led some scholars to describe southwestern humor as an elitist exercise in the mockery of uneducated yeoman. As one critic summarizes this position, "the once-fashionable view of this writing, clabbered up in its inapt metaphor [of *cordon sanitaire* (sanitary cordon or barrier)], is that the Southwestern authors were Whig moralists who tempered their amusement of Democratic hijinks by constructing cautionary tales of warning against uppity illiterates."[23] Recent generations of humor scholars have come to repudiate this account. As closer reading of these stories reveals, the narratives of southwestern humor do not quarantine their narrators; on the contrary, they foreground contact between traveling professionals and rural inhabitants. When genteel narrators reproduce the speech of rustics in print, the resultant "linguistic contamination" of these comedic contact zones makes the narrators sound more like yeomen and the fictional yeomen more genteel and learned. In addition to the stories that he borrowed directly from the southwestern humorists, Lincoln also engaged in the conscious use of "contamination" when telling his jokes and stories. His use of slang and dialect operated simultaneously as raillery and as self-satire, since he performed rusticity

"This Reminds Me of a Little Joke"

while gently mocking it. Even as president, Lincoln responded to "stylish visitors" to the White House with deliberately rustic diction and anecdotes.[24] Through such performances, Lincoln used "linguistic contamination" to mock his visitors for putting on airs while personifying a particularly democratic essence as a representative of the people.

Southwestern humorists' Whiggery, then, should be seen not as class-based elitism but as a good-natured clash between a burgeoning professional class and unlettered settlers in a frontier setting. If southwestern humor was written "largely by a new class of professionals—circuit lawyers, journalists, doctors, shopowners—whose line of work demanded, in ways the landed aristocracy were never bound, that they come into contact with poor whites," Lincoln, as a circuit lawyer and a one-time grocery storekeeper in a frontier town, fit the bill. Further, these authors were professionals who "cast their lot with the future," in contrast to the "unambitious yeomen and marginal settlers" whom they gently ribbed in their writing for their "quirky, complacent individualism" and resistance to the progress of civilization. This is the position that Lincoln held as a young man in New Salem and then Springfield: striving, Whiggish on progress and internal improvements but connected to his yeoman Kentucky and Indiana roots and friendly with the frontier farmers who were his neighbors. He, thus, performed what one scholar of southwestern humor has identified as a key theme of this literature: "backwoods civility," in which the "positive possibilities of frontier folk" are represented in comic ways.[25] Lincoln sought to show that he understood and respected—as people and as voters—western yeoman, even as he gently ribbed them about their aversion to the progress the Whig platform of internal improvements exemplified.

All of this is apparent in one of Lincoln's early political satires, his 1842 "Letter from the Lost Townships" to the editor of the *Sangamo Journal*. In this piece, Lincoln takes on the persona of a farmwife named Rebecca, a character he continued from a previous letter from another author. His tough, folksy female narrator recalls Benjamin Franklin's use of Silence Dogood to satirize public-sphere issues from a position of seemingly uninterested powerlessness.[26] Rebecca's political voice is also reminiscent of southwestern humorist F. M. Noland's Pete Whetstone character, who argues in a plainspoken way for Whig policies. As the title implies, the setting is rural, and Rebecca and her neighbor Jeff see political matters in practical instead of esoteric or ideological terms. Lincoln had long been a staunch defender of banks, which he felt provided an elastic supply of money necessary for economic growth (and, relatedly, internal improvements projects) on the frontier. When the Bank of Illinois failed in 1842, he maintained that defense and blamed deleterious national policies.[27] Whigs like Lincoln lambasted Democratic state auditor James Shields after he decided that state-bank currency would only be accepted at a discount. The pretense for the "Rebecca" letter is to ask the editor whether Shields is a Whig or a Democrat. Jeff launches into a diatribe against "the cursed British whigs," claims to have seen Shields through a window at a Whig event, and rants, "He's a whig, and no mistake: nobody but a whig could make such a conceity dunce of himself." Rebecca responds by pointing out to Jeff that "the proclamation is in your own democratic paper."[28] Lincoln's character, thus, lays blame upon Whigs but mistakenly. The content of Jeff's complaint remains valid, but upon Rebecca's revelation, the perpetrator shifts from Whig to Democrat.

But Jeff, still convinced that Shields is a Whig, wagers on it with Rebecca, who then asks the *Sangamo Journal* to settle the bet. This is the ostensible purpose of the "Rebecca" letter, but Lincoln's persona also gives a second purpose: to "help to send the present hypocritical set to where they belong" and install men who will "take on fewer airs." Hence, the letter seeks to co-opt the position of the common man for political gain. The basis of Jeff's contention that Shields is a Whig is that he is conceited, like Whigs who "wouldn't let no democrats in [to a Whig event], for fear they'd disgust the ladies, or scare the little galls, or dirty the floor."[29] In his satiric equation of Shields and Whiggery, Lincoln reverses common stereotypes about the political parties. That is, in presenting a Democrat as going against the will of common people, especially farmers, the logical assumption was that the Whigs, in their opposition to Democrats, were, therefore, *for* the will of common folk, despite the reputation Jeff imputes to them. "A measure of the effectiveness of Lincoln's satire," one scholar points out, "is that it nearly got him killed." After two other "Rebecca" letters (probably not written by Lincoln), one of which Mary Todd coauthored, Shields demanded the name of the author from the *Journal*'s editor, Simeon Francis, and eventually challenged Lincoln to a duel. This incident brought Lincoln and Todd back into proximity after a previous falling out. In this sense, we can locate satire at the advent not just of Lincoln's political career but also his marriage.[30]

Lincoln wrote many such pieces for several Illinois newspapers and sent reports from the state capital, Springfield, to the *Sangamo Journal* under pseudonyms like Johnny Blubberhead, Sampson's Ghost, and Old Settler.

Though it is impossible to tell for certain which articles are from Lincoln because most such pieces appear anonymously or under pseudonyms, scholars estimate that he authored hundreds. James H. Matheny, a Springfield lawyer who stood in Lincoln's wedding, claimed to have delivered hundreds of editorials from Lincoln to *Sangamo Journal* editor Francis. In Illinois politics as played out in local newspapers, Lincoln was a constant satiric mouthpiece for Whig policies and goader of individual Democratic politicians, whom he lampooned severely. In some of these pieces, Lincoln even posed as prominent Democrats to make them seem silly or incompetent.[31] Though he consistently lambasted Democrats in these articles, as the "Rebecca" letter shows, he did not do so entirely at the expense of yeoman frontiersmen. Here and elsewhere, Lincoln went even further than the southwest humorists in blurring distinctions between backwoodsman and gentleman. In his satires, he gained a laugh at the expense of baffled rubes but employed "backwoods civility" to situate himself through his public persona as empathetic. Lincoln's take on southwestern humor was in a sense a performance of political doublespeak, in which he imbibed the language and interests of Illinois farmers while gently winking at their greenness; his self-deprecation, humble past, and modest demeanor made the satire convivial instead of mean-spirited.

Twenty years later, as President of the United States, Lincoln could little afford to be caught writing snarkily partisan sketches for newspapers, but he did consistently apply the work of other humorists to political situations. Indeed, by reciting and applying his favorite literary comedians, he was able to frame sarcastic critiques through indirection, in effect using them to make points while denying responsibility for the jests' content. Lincoln had plenty of material to choose from. While living in the White House, Lincoln had on hand copies of *Joe Miller's Jests* and Lowell's *Biglow Papers* along with collections of humorous essays and letters from dialect writers Orpheus C. Kerr, pseudonym of R. H. Newell; Artemus Ward, pseudonym of Charles Farrar Browne; and Petroleum V. Nasby, pseudonym of David R. Locke.[32] Lincoln joked to General Montgomery C. Meigs that anyone who hadn't read the *Orpheus C. Kerr Papers* was "a heathen." Lincoln kept and recited these works not simply for comic relief; he also applied their humor to more public discussions on serious political issues. After promoting Grant to lieutenant general, for instance, Lincoln recited to him a fable from Kerr's *Palace Beautiful and Other Poems* about a monkey who thought he would be a great general if only he had a longer (and then longer and then longer) tail, until he collapsed under its weight.[33] Journalist Noah Brooks—an acquaintance from Lincoln's Illinois days and a constant visitor at the White House—claimed that Lincoln carried a Nasby newspaper column about the migration of blacks to Ohio and would recite it to friends and colleagues because he felt that "the feeling of the anti-war and ultra-conservative men was so capitally travestied" in it. According to Locke, editor of the Findlay, Ohio, *Jeffersonian*, Lincoln offered him a political post, "any place you ask for—*that you are capable of filling—and fit to fill*." Locke declined, but this reveals how fully Lincoln mixed his humor and his politics. Even more telling of the political use of humor for Lincoln, soon after Lincoln's death, a copy of *Joe Miller's Jests* was found in his desk drawer, next to important papers.[34]

Lincoln's explanation of Ward's humor is illustrative of how Lincoln viewed and how he used the dialect humorists he so loved. Russell H. Conwell, a Civil War soldier and acquaintance of Lincoln and author of *Why Lincoln Laughed* (1922), claims, "Lincoln said that much of Ward's humor was of the educational sort. It aroused intellectual activity of the finest kind, and he mentioned Ward's constant use of riddles as an illustration. Then he spoke of the ancient Samson riddle and the fables of Aesop, and called attention to the fact that they employed a joke to train the mind by the study of keen satire. He said Ward was like that." Granted, this may be an overzealous appraisal of the quality and depth of Ward's work, but it does show that Lincoln viewed satire as a means of political education, training minds to question the surfaces of what is seen and assumed. Lincoln saw the shaping of public sentiment as a key role of politicians and knew that public opinion was malleable; it was, in the words of one biographer, "susceptible to education and redirection."[35] In redeploying jokes, fables, quotes, and scenes from his favorite humorists as satire, Lincoln was teaching political lessons to his auditors and encouraging them to engage in similar critical thinking.

Jokes on Lincoln's Joking

Of course, not everyone got the joke. Such is the complexity of Lincoln's character and image that he was simultaneously praised as a great dignitary and reviled as a tasteless comedian. Caricaturists and satirists commonly portrayed Lincoln's love of humor as inappropriately frivolous during a solemn and devastating war. Lincoln's love of wit was a key reason for the plethora of caricatures of him.[36]

"This Reminds Me of a Little Joke"

Depictions of Lincoln as a jester began appearing from the beginning of his presidency. In "Great and Astonishing Trick of Old Abe, the Western Juggler," for example, from an 1861 issue of the comic periodical *Frank Leslie's Budget of Fun*, Lincoln is dressed as an entertainer and attempts to swallow the sword of war (fig. 1.2). The cartoon tries to make Lincoln look ridiculous by reducing his attempt to deal with secession to a circus trick. More severe in its criticism of Lincoln the joker is Frank Bellew's "The National Joker," in another humor magazine, *Funniest of Phun*, in September 1864 (fig. 1.3). Here, Lincoln, in a jester outfit and standing in a circus ring, smiles and tells his audience, "This reminds me of a little joke," and "This reminds me of another little story," common attributions to Lincoln in Civil War cartoons to characterize his penchant for telling humorous anecdotes. In drawing the President of the United States in a jester's outfit, Bellew endeavored to demean the president's use of humor as decidedly unpresidential. The horrifying scenes of war pictured in the bubbles overhead—the hospital, Liberty aflame, and the battlefield—imply that Lincoln's humor was in exceedingly poor taste during wartime. Part of this disgust arose from a false but powerful rumor, given credence and currency by being printed in the *New York World*, that Lincoln had made off-color jokes while touring the Antietam battlefield. A similarly damning juxtaposition of the horrors of war and Lincoln's love of humor is at work in printmaker Joseph E. Baker's 1864 lithograph "Columbia Demands Her Children!" (fig. 1.4). In this cartoon, an angry Columbia points accusingly at Lincoln and shouts, "Mr. LINCOLN give me back my 500,000 sons!!!" Lincoln looks nonplussed and sits in a relaxed position at his writing desk, with his right leg slung over the back of his chair. A call for more troops lies on the floor. Searching for an answer, Lincoln says, "Well the fact is—by the way that reminds me of a STORY!!!"[37]

The 1864 poster "I Knew Him, Horatio" uses a Shakespeare allusion to offer a similar critique of Lincoln (fig. 1.5). In this cartoon, General and Democratic presidential nominee George B. McClellan plays the role of Hamlet, holding Lincoln's severed, laughing head and soliloquizing, "I knew him, Horatio; A fellow of infinite jest . . . Where be your gibes now?"[38] The imputation here is that Lincoln's joking will lead to a political death, with McClellan as the benefactor. Unlike pro-Lincoln cartoons that picture a "long Lincoln" to emphasize his staying power, this cartoon repurposes the Hamlet soliloquy to imply the opposite: Lincoln's transience as a one-term president (or so the cartoonist falsely predicts).

Figure 1.2. "Great and Astonishing Trick of Old Abe, the Western Juggler."
Frank Leslie's Budget of Fun, *April 15, 1861, 16. Courtesy, American Antiquarian Society.*

Figure 1.3. "The National Joker." *Frank Bellew,* Funniest of Phun, *September 1864, 16.* HarpWeek.

Figure 1.4. "Columbia Demands Her Children!" Lithograph. *Joseph E. Baker (Boston, 1864). Library of Congress.*

Figure 1.5. "I Knew Him, Horatio." Poster cartoon. *J. H. Howard (New York: Strong, 1864). Library of Congress.*

A potentially self-defeating problem with these cartoon attacks on Lincoln's sense of humor is their context. "The National Joker," for example, appeared in the comic periodical *Funniest of Phun.* Presumably, the readers of this magazine enjoyed humor, even during wartime; the magazine was counting on this fact for its continued existence. As such, its readers would most likely not be the types to impugn Lincoln for having and exercising a sense of humor similar to their own. Political cartoons make light of serious issues and, conversely, use levity to make serious points; the comic periodicals in which many of them appeared worked in the same way, so any critiques within those media of using humor to deal with serious issues likely came off as hypocritical and, thus, probably ineffectual.

Print satires that mocked Lincoln for making jokes faced the same dilemma of hypocrisy. For example, the 1864 campaign song sheet "Hey! Uncle Abe, Are You Joking Yet?" connects Lincoln's humor to abolition: "Honest Old Abe was a queer old coon, / Joked with a nigger and play'd the buffoon." In the pamphlet *Abraham Africanus I, His Secret Life, Revealed under the Mesmeric Influence, Mysteries of the White House* (1864), "Lincoln," narrating his life story while mesmerized, admits, "I learnt my statesmanship from a comic almanac, and got my jokes from an old Joe Miller," and

"This Reminds Me of a Little Joke"

persists in telling jokes even while under hypnosis.[39] New York Democrat J. F. Feeks, who printed both of these pieces, as well as *The Lincoln Catechism* (1864) and *Lincolniana or Humors of Uncle Abe* (1864), also published borrowed jokes; the criticism of Lincoln for doing the same might appear highly disingenuous even to Feeks's partisan readers.

Some criticisms of Lincoln as a clownish leader with a reputation for joking were delivered by characters who were themselves satirized simultaneously. Southwestern humorist Charles H. Smith, writing as Bill Arp, a naive Georgia cracker, published three letters to Lincoln in the Georgia paper *Southern Confederacy* in 1861 and 1862 (collected in book form in 1866). These letters offer friendly but demeaning advice and satirize Arp's misunderstanding of politics and geography as well as the North's lack of progress in the war. In one letter, Arp invites Lincoln and Seward to come visit him "so we can fix up and swap a lie or two with you." Here Arp figures Lincoln as a fellow southwestern humorist, able to give and take in the telling of tall tales for amusement. In another letter, Arp sarcastically lauds Lincoln's standing as a comic and even offers advice in preserving his witticisms for posterity: "I would like to see you personally, Mr. Lincoln, and hear you talk and tell some of your funny anecdotes, like you told Governor Morehead [former Kentucky governor, present for the "Lion and the Woodsman's Daughter" fable]. I laughed when I read them till the tears fairly rained from my eyelids—I know I could make my fortune, Mr. Lincoln, compiling your wit. May I be your Boswell, and follow you about?"[40] In claiming to be Lincoln's compatriot as a humorist, the obviously flawed Arp denigrates Lincoln as a vulgar joker by bringing him down to Arp's own level. But, again, the readers of Smith's Bill Arp letters enjoyed humor during the war, even humor about the war, which is what Arp's letters to Lincoln mostly traffic in.

Even if they hated the man, Southern readers seem to have relished Lincoln's jokes. After all, even Confederate publications circulated comic anecdotes under Lincoln's name. The humor magazine *Southern Punch*, for instance, repeated several jokes that it attributed to Lincoln, including the following: "Old Abe, in discussing the political polygamic interests of Utah, is said to have remarked: 'It is all nonsense to talk about polygamy. I know, from experience, that one wife at a time is as much as any man can get along with.'"[41] This is a nonpartisan, nonsectional joke, with one butt located far away, in Utah, and the other, Mary Todd Lincoln, in the White House; it, therefore, associates Lincoln with laughter in a harmless light (aside from its sexism) that belies attempts to render a negative image of Lincoln's joking.

In the Northern comic press, *Frank Leslie's Budget of Fun* included a satire on Lincoln in the May 1, 1861, issue that chided him early in his presidency for his penchant for joking. In a fake letter to the editors, "Lincoln" tells a poor joke and says, "You can judge by this that I'm just the right one to appreciate your Budget, and that there's a sort of federal feeling between us." Finally, he leads up to his reason for writing: to ask advice on national policy. "Lincoln" explains, "Splitting sides is one thing, splitting rails is also one thing, if it isn't anything else—but splitting up these great United States is another thing, and no mistake." The *Budget* editors' reply takes Lincoln to task for his claims as a humorist: "Our dear and incompetent old friend, we enclose you fifty cents for that weak joke. . . . You may do very well for a dismembered President, but leave joking alone; you don't know enough, and never will." This insult implies not that humor is particularly distasteful or beneath his office but, rather, that Lincoln is beneath humor, which requires a ready wit that Lincoln lacks. The *Budget* then offers the following political advice: "remember that you are legislating for white people." This suggestion hints at the periodical's underlying, racist reason for its criticisms of Lincoln. Indeed, the *Budget* was consistently suspicious of abolitionism even as it tempered its denunciations of Lincoln after his election and Southern secession.[42]

Later in the year, the *Budget* editors saw the need to justify their own use of humor during the war. The front page of the November 1861 issue lays out reasons to be jocular during times when the "World" is "in its most serious mood": "a little comic emollient," the *Budget* claims, can "make the great cogwheels move more easily; or, to serve up the same thought in a different shape—a cheerful face and voice are godsends . . . in that great mourning-coach, the Republic." Lincoln, too, cited as an animus for his humor "the desire to bring cheer to others" during wartime.[43] The *Budget*, then, found itself in the position of claiming the usefulness and even the necessity of what it chided Lincoln for doing.

Some humor publications avoided such hypocrisy by depicting Lincoln's levity as a necessary and humane response during a tragic period in American history. One pro-Lincoln joke book—*Old Abe's Jokes, Fresh from Abraham's Bosom* (1864)—rationalizes Lincoln's humor by contextualizing it within the pressures and responsibilities of his office: "It would be hardly necessary to inform the nation that our President, in the midst of the anxieties of a state of war that continually torture his mind, is wont to find occasional relief in an appropriate anecdote or well-turned jest."

　　　　　　　　　　　　　"This Reminds Me of a Little Joke"

Of course, T. R. Dawley, "Publisher for the Millions" and of this book of Abraham Lincoln jokes, had a particular pecuniary interest in convincing readers that it was safe to laugh, both for the president and for the people. But *Old Abe's Jokes*, which combines standard jokes attributed to Lincoln with a biography and several heartwarming stories of Lincoln's kindness and compassion, goes further than merely apologizing for Lincoln's humor. This is most evident in the entry "'Salmon the Solemn,' vs. Abraham the Jocular." The comparison attacks Lincoln's Secretary of Treasury Salmon P. Chase's underhanded presidential aspirations, describing him as unqualified for the presidency because he was *not humorous enough*:

> The solemn versus the jocular are brought into curious juxtaposition by the present state of affairs. The committee of "the friends of Mr. Chase," in their Ohio circular, call Mr. Lincoln "our jocular President." Against him they set up Mr. Chase, of whom a prominent Boston lawyer said some years ago, "I don't like the Governor. He is too solemn—altogether too solemn." More than a year ago, Mr. Lincoln said that he had just discovered that the initials of Salmon P. Chase mean shinplaster currency [a nineteenth-century epithet for bank notes and other paper currency]. Perhaps he will now say that they mean shinplaster candidate. An old Greek rhetorician advises to answer your adversary's sober arguments with ridicule, and his ridicule with sober argument.[44]

This example, more sarcastic retort than joke, seems to equate statesmanship with humor as a way of defending, and reversing, charges that Lincoln's joking was a sign of his unfitness for office. "This Reminds Me of a Little Joke" (fig. 1.6) attributes to Lincoln the same dialogue line as does "The National Joker" but "This Reminds Me" uses it to opposite effect. That is, instead of figuring Lincoln's jocularity as crude and misplaced, this image pictures humor as political power, as a gigantic Lincoln holds his Democratic opponent, the diminutive McClellan, in the palm of his hand. Lincoln, the cartoon hints, could afford to joke about his opponents, so long as he fulfilled the duties of his office. As he makes the comment, "This reminds me of a little joke," Lincoln is seated at his desk, which implies that his verbal play is part of his job as president. McClellan is no more than a tiny plaything, his campaign's challenge to Lincoln's reelection a mere "joke."[45]

Figure 1.6. "This Reminds Me of a Little Joke." *Frank Bellew,* Harper's Weekly, *September 17, 1864, 608. Courtesy, American Antiquarian Society.*

Bellew, the artist who created this image, also drew "The National Joker" (see fig. 1.3); the cartoons, both of which put the same words in Lincoln's mouth, appeared during the same month in different periodicals. In crafting two very different Lincoln images—one celebratory and one denunciatory, each using the same line of dialogue—Bellew drew upon the appropriability of visual and verbal signs and the competing political uses to which symbols and utterances can be put.[46]

Satire in Circulation: Lincoln as Comic Currency

A comparison of pro-Lincoln and anti-Lincoln joke books provides another example of how artists and audiences drew (or tried to draw) antithetical conclusions from the same comic evidence. As Zall points out, "Both parties capitalized on his fame for funny stories—Democrats in mockery, Republicans in praise of his homely humanity."[47] What he does not mention is that such "praise" and "mockery" often arose from the same jokes. For

"This Reminds Me of a Little Joke"

example, *Old Abe's Jokes*, the anti-Lincoln *Lincolniana, or Humors of Uncle Abe* (1864, published by Feeks, fig. 1.7), and the seemingly politically neutral *Old Abe's Joker, or Wit at the White House* (1863; fig. 1.8) share, almost verbatim, several jokes and "Lincoln stories." One example, which appears in all three books, is a joke attributed to Lincoln about congressmen. "A Comparison" is from *Lincolniana.*

One day as Uncle Abe, and a friend were sitting on the House of Representatives steps, the session closed, and the members filed out in a body. Uncle Abe looked after them with a serious smile. "That reminds me," said he, "of a little incident when I was a boy; my flat boat lay up at Alton on the Mississippi, for a day, and I strolled about the town. I saw a large stone building, with massive stone walls, not so handsome though, as this, and while I was looking at it, the iron gateway opened, and a great body of men came out." "What do you call that?" I asked a bystander. "That," said he, "is the State Prison, and those are all thieves going home. Their time is up."

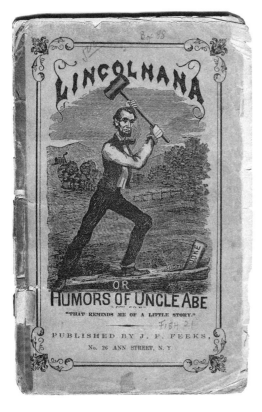

Figure 1.7. *Lincolniana, or Humors of Uncle Abe.* Cover. *Andrew Adderup (New York: Feeks, 1864). Abraham Lincoln Presidential Library and Museum.*

Old Abe's Jokes offers the same story, called "Old Abe on the Congressmen": the only differences are in wording. Lincoln is, more reverentially, called "the President" and then "Abraham" and is credited with a "sardonic" smile as he tells the story. The version in *Old Abe's Joker*, also called "Old Abe on the Congressmen," follows that in *Old Abe's Jokes* almost exactly but makes it more immediate by beginning "The other day."[48] Such repetition, like Bellew's multipurpose caption, shows that critics and supporters used essentially the same version of Lincoln to chastise or celebrate him. It is the introductory matter that distinguishes these joke books as pro-Lincoln, anti-Lincoln, or neutral; the jokes themselves are the same. These productions, it seems, utilize Lincoln as a marketing tool and a well-known reference point to connect popular humor to national politics.

A parallel instance of the same Lincoln jokes being offered with different political intentions occurred in February 1864, when the *New York Post* printed multiple columns of "Several Little Stories by or about President Lincoln." The *New York Herald* immediately mocked the *Post* (which had

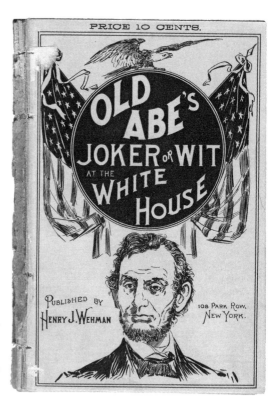

Figure 1.8. *Old Abe's Joker, or Wit at the White House.* Cover. *New York: Wehman, 1863. Abraham Lincoln Presidential Library and Museum.*

"This Reminds Me of a Little Joke"

not yet endorsed Lincoln's reelection) by reprinting "Several Little Stories," with the subhead, "The Presidential Campaign: The First Electioneering Document. The *Evening Post* Out in Favor of 'Old Abe.'"[49] The same Lincoln jokes were used as column filler but also as sallies in a politically tinged, internecine newspaper war. Once again, it is the introductory material, not the jokes themselves, that announces the particular political stance.

Lincoln's persona was also widely circulated as cultural currency entirely without political affiliation. Popular-culture producers took advantage of Lincoln's zest for humor to sell books, pamphlets, almanacs, prints, and other products. *Old Abe's Joker, or Wit at the White House*, for instance, uses Lincoln's name in its title and his image on its cover yet includes no more than ten Lincoln jokes or stories in the entire book (the joke discussed above being one example). The book's preface as much as admits this, asking, "What could be more natural than to associate with 'quips and cranks and wanton wiles,' the name of one who so greatly enjoys and successfully perpetrates the fine old, full-flavored joke[?]"[50] In essence, the joke book does no more than "associate" apolitical jokes with Lincoln's name. *Uncle Abe's Comic Almanac, 1865* (1864) similarly leverages Lincoln's fame as a satirist-statesman without entering the satiric fray at all. Here again, Lincoln is featured in the title and on the cover, but the comic almanac contains *no* mention of Lincoln or even of the still-raging Civil War.

As Lincoln and his humorous stories were appropriated for different purposes by parties at all points on the ideological spectrum of mid-nineteenth-century America, so, too, did Lincoln engage in politically motivated cultural appropriations. Symbols, of course, "can be seized . . . and turned against those who last appropriated them," and Lincoln was astutely aware of the importance of redefining the content of cultural symbols. This is precisely what he did, for example, after the fall of Richmond in the spring of 1865, when a crowd gathered outside the White House and shouted for the president. Lincoln emerged at the window, told the crowd that he would forgo a speech, and, instead, asked the band to play the "captured" tune of "Dixie." He jokingly justified his request: "I have always thought 'Dixie' one of the best tunes I have ever heard. Our adversaries over the way attempted to appropriate it, but I insisted yesterday that we fairly captured it. [*Applause.*] I presented the question to the Attorney General, and he gave it as his legal opinion that it is our lawful prize. [*Laughter and applause.*] I now request the band to favor me with its performance." In making this request—note especially his tongue-in-cheek uses of the terms "appropriate," "captured," and "lawful prize"—Lincoln displayed his highly developed consciousness of the ideological importance of cultural symbols and especially their openness to ironic appropriation and redefinition. This was not a one-time effusion in response to good news from the front; rather, Lincoln throughout his political career operated through oppositional reoccupation of prevailing symbols and sly deflection of criticisms. As this shows, the "fluidity" of symbols does not render them meaningless or undecidable. On the contrary, "the undecidability of discourse is always, at least in certain hands, very much to the political point . . . because its undecidability makes it always open to interested appropriation."[51] Lincoln himself was an "interested" appropriator and made shrewd political use of the fluidity of the affective content of traditional political symbols.

Lincoln seems not only to have been the object of humorous circulation but also, at times, its source. His secretary John Hay, who spread administration opinions by writing as a "special correspondent" for newspapers from Washington, D.C., to St. Louis, Missouri, likely provided some of the "Several Little Stories" (discussed above) to the *New York Post*. Hay also corresponded often with his friend Colonel Charles Graham Halpine (aka the satiric poetic persona Miles O'Reilly), an officer and humor columnist for the *New York Herald*, offering gossip and humorous anecdotes for Halpine's satires. For example, Hay wrote Halpine in August 1863 seeking inside information on the political mood in New York City: "I know of no man upon whose statements I can so entirely rely as upon yours about New York matters. I wish you would write me as fully as you can about the real feeling and sentiment there about the conscription: What sort of a party the News represents, if any at all and what is the real strength of factions there. Your communications shall be held strictly confidential as to yourself and only used for the information of the President in any case." Halpine, in return, wanted humorous anecdotes and bon mots from the president and other administration officials to include in his columns, most famously his O'Reilly satires, printed first in the *New York Herald* and then in book form as *The Life and Adventures, Songs, Services, and Speeches of Private Miles O'Reilly* (1864). These poems make use of Lincoln's love of wit as a touchstone and raison d'être for the narrative of the fictional Irish poet O'Reilly. According to the story tying together the O'Reilly songs, O'Reilly was a navy seaman arrested for printing and disseminating one of his songs, most of which are military satires lampooning officers, battles, and the like. But, the story goes, Lincoln pardoned O'Reilly upon witnessing his performance in the

Oval Office of "Sambo's Right to Be Kilt," a song about African American troops in the Union army. O'Reilly then produced a "thank-you" song for Lincoln that both praised and teased him.

> Though thraitors abused him vilely,
> He was honest an' kindly, he loved a joke,
> An' he pardoned Miles O'Reilly
>
> . . .
>
> If you ain't the handsomest man in the world
> You've done handsome by me, an' highly;
> And your name to postherity will go down
> Arm in arm wid Miles O'Reilly.[52]

For Halpine, having a satirist in the White House gave a kind of official sanction to satirize the war, as symbolized in Lincoln's pardon. Such satirists brought the "National Joker" into their productions as a fellow comedian, part of the joke. This affinity with other satirists is another reason why the Lincoln image was so difficult to assail satirically.

Halpine was particularly interested in hearing from Hay how administration officials had responded to the O'Reilly satires, hoping to incorporate those reactions into subsequent pieces. This demonstrates the close connections between the Lincoln's administration and satires on it, as well as the sometimes inextricable nature of satiric fictions and their real-life referents. Halpine couched his request to Hay in purely political terms on November 18, 1863.

> Private Miles is about to visit Washn. And be introduced to the
> Prest., of whom for reelection (*vide* Herald passim) he is a warm
> and devoted supporter. Have you any annecdote [*sic*] you could
> give me of what *anybody* said about Miles? . . . *Any* annecdote [*sic*]
> from the Presdt. if new would be worth its weight in gold. . . . I
> promise if you help me in this my hour of need that OReilly will be
> discreet and give you no cause to blush for him. . . . Can you give
> me any *fresh saying* or *annecdote* [*sic*] of the Prest. No matter what it
> may be, it can be worked in. Anything like his "plowing round the
> stumps that couldn't be either grubbed or burnt out," with which
> I commenced my article on Jim Lane and the Kansas Missouri
> troubles some five or six weeks ago. Mr [*James Gordon*] Bennet
> wishes the next OReilly paper on the Presidency and to be a strong
> political & Irish document for Mr. Lincoln.

In this letter Halpine sought new material—specifically, Lincoln anecdotes and his administration's reaction to previous satires—for his O'Reilly series, which he promised Hay he would use to promote instead of denigrate the president during the upcoming campaign. In his response, Hay reported his attempts to secure new material for Halpine by "skulking in the shadow of the Tycoon, setting all sorts of dextrous [sic] traps for a joke, telling good stories myself to draw him out and suborning [secretary John] Nicolay to aid in the foul conspiracy." He then offered one Lincoln bon mot but encouraged Halpine "not to use it" because the anecdote was "blasphemous" and might "hurt the 'Quaker vote.'" Halpine used it anyway.[53] Whether Hay was serious in his caution to Halpine, their friendship seems to have facilitated a pipeline of humorous anecdotes from Lincoln to the press. Hay's and Halpine's letters reveal a symbiotic political relationship: each seeking insider information from the other, Halpine requesting "authentic" Lincoln material to enliven his satires and Hay working to preserve his boss's dignity in the press and simultaneously circulating his humor, thus augmenting Lincoln's reputation as a joker while leveraging it for voter appeal and to broadcast political points.

Possibly, the most trenchant example of Lincoln's circulation of himself as comic currency is on display in "The President's Last, Shortest, and Best Speech" (Lincoln's title), in which he leveraged his reputation as a humorist in order to illustrate to a national audience why the war was being fought. Noah Brooks recalled that Lincoln sent for him, handed him a short speech, and said, "Here is one speech of mine which has never been printed, and I think it worth printing. Just see what you think." Brooks duly had the anecdote printed in the *Washington, D.C., Daily Chronicle* on December 7, 1864. The story, in its entirety, appears as follows:

On thursday of last week two ladies from Tennessee came before the President asking the release of their husbands held as prisoners of war at Johnson's Island. They were put off till friday, when they came again; and were again put off to saturday. At each of the interviews one of the ladies urged that her husband was a religious man. On saturday the President ordered the release of the prisoners, and then said to this lady "You say your husband is a religious man; tell him when you meet him, that I say I am not much of a judge of religion, but that, in my opinion, the religion that sets men to rebel and fight against their government, because, as they think, that government

"This Reminds Me of a Little Joke"

does not sufficiently help *some* men to eat their bread on the sweat of *other* men's faces, is not the sort of religion upon which people can get to heaven!"

Lincoln's story about himself, written in the third person, uses wit to interrogate the logic of deeply held assumptions. It is not a joke per se but takes the form of a joke, with the president's redescription of the rebellion as its punch line. Even as he put into practice his Reconstruction policy of magnanimity by authorizing the prisoners' release, he assailed them for having bought into an ideology that denied (and required others to assist in that denial) other human beings the opportunities for self-making of which Lincoln had taken such advantage. As Lincoln probably hoped, the piece was reprinted widely, as its brevity made it perfect filler for editorial pages.[54] Such shrewdness shows that Lincoln knew both how to use his reputation as a joker to his own advantage and how to portray a particular type of wit—moral instead of vulgar, humanely invested in the war instead of laughing at it—to the American public.

Of course, Lincoln would use his line about men eating "their bread on the sweat of *other* men's faces," a keen reversal of Genesis 3:19, three months later, in his second inaugural address on March 4, 1865. In that speech Lincoln said, "It may seem strange that any men should dare to ask a just God's assistance in wringing their bread from the sweat of other men's faces; but let us judge not that we be not judged."[55] Lincoln's reuse of a punch line from a widely distributed joke in a serious speech reveals how integral satire was to his political communication.

It also shows, once again, the astuteness of Lincoln's image consciousness and press savvy. Lincoln understood the importance of the press from the beginning to the end of his political career: from his informal education with newspapers while he served as postmaster of New Salem, Illinois, to his service as an anonymous correspondent covering the Illinois legislature in which he served to the days when, as president, he would step outside the White House to ask pedestrians to send nearby newsboys to his front door. Lincoln's law partner William H. Herndon and his writing partner Jesse W. Weik describe Lincoln as a "careful and patient reader of newspapers," and another Lincoln scholar labels him as "what would be called today a newspaper junkie." This experience with and love for newspapers led Lincoln to use them to achieve his political goals. But part of Lincoln's press savvy inhered in his ability to repurpose humorous bits *from* the media, refigure them for satiric purposes, and recirculate them *in* the media, and, thus, participate in and benefit from the nineteenth century's "culture of reprinting."[56] Lincoln's rearticulations of his humorous borrowings changed their meaning in important ways, making the apolitical precisely but still comically political while educating the voting public and public servants alike through satiric indirection.

CHAPTER 2

"Little Big Man":
Modesty and Attack
in Lincoln's Writings
and Speeches

[T]he use of degrading figures is a game at which they
[Democrats] may not find themselves able to take all the
winnings.

—Lincoln, speech in the U.S. House of
Representatives, July 27, 1848

In the biographical sketch that he wrote (in the third person) about himself
for the 1860 presidential campaign, Lincoln was quite candid about his lack
of education. After a brief family genealogy, he detailed the physical labor
that constituted much of his youth, writing that until "his twentythird
[*sic*] year, he was almost constantly handling that most useful instrument
[an ax]—less, of course, in plowing and harvesting seasons." He then
contrasted his laboring experience with his paucity of formal education.

A. now thinks that the agregate of all his schooling did not amount
to one year. He was never inside of a college or Academy as a student;
and never inside a college or accademy building till since he had a
law-license. What he has in the way of education, he has picked up.
After he was twentythree, and had separated from his father, he
studied English grammar, imperfectly of course, but so as to speak
and write as well as he now does. He studied and nearly mastered the

Six-books of Euclid, since he was a member of Congress. He regrets his want of education, and does what he can to supply the want. In his tenth year he was kicked by a horse, and apparantly killed for a time.[1]

The comic juxtaposition here between his lack of education and being "kicked by a horse" is striking, especially considering that Lincoln took great care in preparing his written and spoken texts. Readers of this biography likely expected further Franklinian specifics on Lincoln's self-education and his continuing efforts to "supply the want" but, instead, were jarred by the homey incongruity of a typical rural accident that left him "apparantly" killed for a time.

Was Lincoln in this context offering a joking excuse for stupidity or undermining the myth of the self-made man that was so central to the success of his campaign? Elsewhere in the biography, Lincoln highlighted his several failures, including his time running a dry-goods store, which "winked out." "Of course," Lincoln said of himself and his partner, "they did nothing but get deeper and deeper in debt." Such self-depictions led one historian to label Lincoln "a busted storekeeper and out-of-office Whig."[2] Whether or not Lincoln would agree with this assessment, his campaign autobiography exemplifies the self-deprecating humor that pervaded his thought, speech, and writing.

Such self-mockery was not merely harmless modesty; rather, throughout his career, Lincoln carved out for himself a position of seemingly innocuous powerlessness from which to launch satiric critiques of his opponents and their policies. From this ostensibly demeaned position, Lincoln could attack his opponents' strengths, such as their claims to greatness, heroism, and experience, which he portrayed as antithetical to his own and the American populace's. This is an example of what theorist Michel de Certeau has labeled "tactics," modes and moments of resistance to entrenched professionalism and power.[3] Lincoln's tactics leveraged a consciously performed satiric modesty. His consistent rhetorical alignments of himself with the common and powerless and his renderings of opponents as professionals or "great" men opened up a space for satiric political critique, which Lincoln then delivered through parodic ridicule.

Thomas Ford, governor of Illinois from 1842 to 1846, coined the term "little big man" to describe local politicians who saw themselves as superior to their constituents as well as their opponents. "[A]lmost every neighborhood," he claimed in his 1854 *History of Illinois*, has some one richer than the rest, who puts on airs of importance, and manifests such a want of sympathy with his fellows, as to disgust his humbler neighbors; amongst whom there are those who, full of ill-nature, look upon such pretensions with envious resentment. These little big men, on both sides, of the neighborhood sort . . . think they are devoted to a cause, when they only hate an opponent; and the more thoroughly they hate, the more thoroughly are they partisans. Here originates the hostility between democracy and aristocracy, as it is said to exist in this country.

Robert Bray, in his discussion of Lincoln's early-career use of satire and invective, borrows the term "little big man" to characterize Lincoln's rhetorical tactics as an "underdog strategy." Bray notes that Lincoln positioned "himself in a putatively invidious position with respect to an opponent" and then employed "verbal prowess as the social and political equalizer, cutting the other down to . . . 'little big man' size."[4] Also important is Lincoln's strategic use of self-satire to set up such comparisons, thereby identifying himself with the "common man" and challenging demagogic notions of "greatness" as embodied in politicians. In his speeches, writings, and self-presentation, Lincoln defended himself from criticism by criticizing himself, strategically occupying the ground of ridicule before his opponents could, thereby defining the terms and range of such criticisms.

It was as a verbal satirist that Lincoln most fully forged his distinct brand of political discourse with its novel combination of humility and invective. Apparently, Lincoln's dual predilections for public speaking and satire developed early and concurrently. One of Lincoln's boyhood acquaintances recollected Lincoln's skill at burlesque sermons and speeches: "The boys took turns mounting a stump or box, taking a text—not necessarily from the Bible—, and holding forth so long as the crowd would permit. A man had to be good to last long and most of then [sic] did not last. Lincoln was the favorite 'preacher!' His audience declared he was better than the real preacher. Lincoln often spoke on political topics too, but these talks were often burlesques of political speeches he had heard." As this remembrance shows, Lincoln early associated political and satiric discourse. Biographers William H. Herndon and Jesse W. Weik describe him as an "unequalled" mimic; using his uncanny impersonation skills, Lincoln from his early days used mockery to undercut others' pretensions.[5] As he developed his political and oratorical skills, this association would pay political dividends.

One such example occurred in a January 11, 1837, speech at the legislature in which Lincoln attacked his opponent Usher F. Linder, politicians in general, and, in a self-aware manner, himself in a discussion of the state-bank issue. When banks suspended specie payments, Lincoln sought to defend the banking system against opponents, such as Linder, who represented growing suspicion of the Bank of Illinois and accused bank commissioners of breaking the law (indeed, the Bank of Illinois had made it extremely difficult for citizens to redeem notes, since those notes were redeemable only at the particular branch that had issued them).[6] Lincoln characterized agitation for the creation of a committee to investigate state-bank practices as "exclusively the work of politicians; a set of men who have interests aside from the interests of the people, and who, to say the most of them, are, taken as a mass, at least one long step removed from honest men. I say this with the greater freedom because, being a politician myself, none can regard it as personal." Bray correctly concludes, "Lincoln's disarming inclusion of himself in the class forestalls the opposition's cry of 'you're another,' even as it effectively places the speaker above the tribe's miserable venality and hypocrisy." But Lincoln's humorous self-inclusion also made him a "satirist-satirized" because he had become "self-conscious of his own activity" in admitting that "his own place as a judging and observing subject" was not above implication and, as a result, "reckon[ed] himself into" the satiric critique.[7] In other words, it takes one to know one, as Lincoln's admonition to politicians implies. In Lincoln's case, his self-awareness humorously signaled his understanding of the complexity of issues at stake and, thus, sanctioned his satiric critique. This inclusion of himself in his satiric reproofs disarmed the audience, preemptively denying a counterattack by assuring his auditors that the critique was thorough, thoughtfully self-searching, and honest.

Lincoln deployed "modest satire" via Socratic irony, taking what Aristotle described as an *eiron* stance of (sometimes false) modesty in order to expose his political enemies as *alazons*, or braggarts.[8] Lincoln employed this tactic time and time again in his pre-presidential orations. For example, in opposing Linder's resolution "to institute an enquiry into the management of the affairs of the State Bank," Lincoln feigned trepidation in his January 11, 1837, speech.

> Before I proceed to the body of the subject, I will further remark, that it is not without a considerable degree of apprehension, that I venture to cross the track of the gentleman from Coles (Mr. Linder). Indeed, I do

"Little Big Man"

not believe I could muster a sufficiency of courage to come in contact with that gentleman, were it not for the fact, that he, some days since, most graciously condescended to assure us that he would never be found wasting ammunition on *small game*. On the same fortunate occasion, he further gave us to understand, that he regarded *himself* as being decidedly the *superior* of our common friend from Randolph (Mr. Shields); and feeling, as I really do, that I, to say the most of myself, am nothing more than the peer of our friend from Randolph, I shall regard the gentleman from Coles as decidedly my superior also, and consequently, in the course of what I shall have to say, whenever I shall have occasion to allude to that gentleman, I shall endeavor to adopt that kind of court language which I understand to be due to *decided superiority*.

Lincoln ironically demeaned himself, pretending to take solace in the fact that Linder would consider him small game and, in order to highlight Linder's pretentiousness, went so far as to speak of and to Linder only in what a lowly fellow like Lincoln would assume to be "court language." Indeed, Lincoln referred to Linder as "the gentleman from Coles" through the entirety of the speech. Halfway through, Linder appealed to the house, complaining about Lincoln's tone, but then withdrew the appeal before the question was put, saying that "he preferred to let the gentleman go on; he thought he would break his own neck." In his reply, Lincoln kept to his subject: "Another *gracious condescension*. I acknowledge it with gratitude."[9]

Lincoln's ultimate rhetorical goal in this speech was to undermine the notion of Linder's superiority that Lincoln erected ironically at the outset: "In one faculty, at least, there can be no dispute of the gentleman's superiority over me, and most other men; and that is, the faculty of entangling a subject, so that neither himself, or any other man, can find head or tail to it."[10] The superiority he had been describing, then, was suddenly not something to which anyone would aspire, being re-rendered as incompetence. In this way, Lincoln launched an ad hominem attack through the indirection of ironic praise and false modesty. Or, in terms of classical notions of irony, he played the eiron to demean himself so as to expose Linder as a braggartly alazon. In doing so, he tactically turned Linder's advantages in prestige and experience against him.

Lincoln had done something similar a year earlier on the campaign trail in reply to George Forquer, a respected, older lawyer of distinction and a Whig-turned-Democrat, who, it happens, had installed a lightning rod over his house, which was the nicest in town. Forquer replied to a speech of Lincoln, "This young man will have to be taken down" and, according to Lincoln's friend Joshua Speed, proceeded to give a speech "in a style which, while it was able and fair, in his whole manner asserted and claimed superiority." As Speed remembered it, Lincoln answered,

> The gentleman commenced his speech by saying that this young man would have to be taken down, alluding to me; I am not so young in years as I am in the tricks and trades of a politician; but live long, or die young, I would rather die now, than, like the gentleman change my politics, and simultaneous with the change, receive an office worth three thousand dollars per year, and then have to erect a lightning-rod over my house, to protect a guilty conscience from an offended God.

As in his "skinning of Linder," Lincoln, who had also lambasted Forquer as "King George" and "the royal George" to imply that he was aristocratically out of touch, complimented him as a "gentleman," contrasted with Lincoln's own youthful ambition seeking but having not yet earned "place and distinction." Also like his rejoinder to Linder a year later, Lincoln decried and distanced himself from the "tricks and trades of politicians" before painting Forquer as just such an unscrupulous politician willing to sell his party allegiance for money. Lincoln ended with a punch line that refigured Forquer's well-known status symbol—his lightning rod—as a desperate protective measure against comeuppance for political sins. According to Herndon, "the effect of this rejoinder was wonderful, and gave Forquer and his lightning rod a notoriety the extent of which no one envied him."[11]

Lincoln engaged in the same tactic in 1840 through performance instead of speech. As James H. Matheny remembered the incident in 1866, Lincoln badly humiliated Democrat Colonel E. D. Taylor during the 1840 presidential campaign. Taylor, according to Herndon and Weik, "was a showy, bombastic man, with a weakness for fine clothes and other personal adornments. Frequently he was pitted against Lincoln, and indulged in many bitter flings at the lordly ways and aristocratic pretensions of the Whigs. He had a way of appealing to 'his horny-handed neighbors,' and resorted to many other artful tricks of a demagogue." While Taylor was in the midst of dismissing all Whigs as aristocratic, Lincoln "felt develish" and "moved up to Taylor inch by inch—Lincoln raised slightly up—Caught

"Little Big Man"

Dick Taylors vest corner—gave it a quick jerk—it unbuttoned and out fell Dick ruffle shirt like a pile of Entrails—Swung out to the wind—gold chains—gold watches with large seals hung heavily & massively down." The colonel's hypocrisy thus materially exposed, the entire crowd burst into "furious & uproarious laughter."[12] This performance satire functioned in much the same way as Lincoln's dismantling of Linder by building him up. In visually demonstrating the disconnect between Taylor's rhetoric and his personal attire and deportment, Lincoln undercut the grounds of Taylor's self-righteousness and rebutted his accusations against Whigs, all without saying a single word. This incident also demonstrates Lincoln's keen awareness of the power of symbols, an insight that would serve him well in his later political life.

Lincoln followed up his visual satire with a stark verbal comparison. He said, as Ninian W. Edwards, Illinois politician and husband to Mary Todd's sister, recalled it,

> whilst Col. Taylor had his stores over the country, and was riding in a fine carriage, wore his kid cloves [gloves] and had a gold headed cane, he was a poor boy hired on a flat boat at eight dollars a month, and had only one pair of breeches and they were of buckskin now said he if you know the nature of buckskin when wet and dried by the sun they would shrink and mine kept shrinking until they left for several inches my legs bare between the top of my Socks and the lower part of my breeches—and whilst I was growing taller they were becoming shorter: and so much tighter, that they left a blue streak around my leg which you can see to this day—If you call this aristocracy I plead guilty to the charge.[13]

Like in his "Rebecca" satire, Lincoln here turned the tables on Democratic accusations of Whigs as aristocrats. Starkly contrasting their backgrounds through clothing in a way that belittled Lincoln himself as a comic character with too-short breeches and stained legs, thus mocking the notion of "blue blood," Lincoln again ingratiated himself with his audience by exploiting his opponent's pretensions to superiority.

Lincoln's homespun Whig forebear, Tennessee backwoodsman-turned-congressman David Crockett, recounted pulling a similar stunt against a political opponent who attempted to degrade him in the House of Representatives by mocking his rural roots, referring to him as the "gentleman from the cane." To get his revenge, Crockett allegedly found in the dust a cambric ruffle of precisely the cut affected by Mr. M——l. This he pinned to his own coarse shirt. Choosing a dramatically propitious moment just after the House had attended informative remarks from Mr. M——l, he arose as though to express his own opinion on the matter. The cambric ruffle stood out on David's rough shirt like a light on a locomotive. Suddenly the humor of the situation burst upon all the members at once. Without a word's being uttered, the House burst into prolonged laughter. Mr. M——l hesitated for a single embarrassed moment, then precipitately withdrew from the chamber amid a rising roar.[14]

As Lincoln would do to Taylor, Crockett engaged in physical comedy to expose the pretentiousness of his opponent's dress and bearing. Lincoln shared with Crockett this penchant for visual pillory and, in his early career anyway, a taste for retributative satire that ridiculed the aristocratic affectations of others while embracing a particularly homespun manner and political identity.

This novel combination of politics and levity was as effective as it was crowd-pleasing; or, rather, it was effective because it was crowd-pleasing. John M. Scott, an Illinois attorney, Lincoln contemporary, and, eventually, chief justice of the Illinois Supreme Court, explained that in Lincoln's 1840 campaign stumping, "much time was devoted to telling stories to illustrate some phase of his argument, but more often the telling of these stories was resorted to for the purpose of rendering his opponents ridiculous." Such a style, Scott later recalled, was "much appreciated at that early day," and Lincoln "had no equals in the state" at telling humorous anecdotes that put "the opposing party and its speakers in a most ludicrous position" and "gave him a most favorable hearing for the arguments he later made in support of the measures he was sustaining." This was not, Scott admitted, a particularly "fair mode of treating an adversary," but it was a "mode of attack greatly relished by popular assemblies" because "most people like to see their opponents discomfited by being the butt of a well told story."[15]

Of course, such shenanigans—physical and verbal—left Lincoln open to charges of cruelty and immaturity. The November 23, 1839, *Illinois State Register*, published in Springfield, warned Lincoln in a review of one of his speeches against continuing "a sort of *assumed clownishness*" in his political speech: "Mr. Lincoln will sometimes make his language correspond with this clownish manner, and he can thus frequently raise a loud laugh among his Whig hearers; but this entire game of buffoonery convinces the *mind* of no man, and is utterly lost on the majority of his audience." The article went on to advise Lincoln "to correct this clownish fault before it grows upon him."[16] The charge here was not necessarily that Lincoln's use of humor and satire—which he would continue to deploy voluminously during the ensuing 1840 presidential campaign—was unprofessional so much as that it was ineffective. Lincoln seemed to take this or similar advice to heart as he honed his political rhetoric over the next twenty years.

He learned this lesson more fully after an incident in 1840 in which he impersonated and ridiculed Democrat Jesse B. Thomas so vindictively that Thomas was reduced to tears. According to Herndon, the "'skinning' of Thomas . . . was not soon forgotten either by his friends or enemies. I heard him afterwards say that the recollection of his conduct that evening filled him with the deepest chagrin. He felt that he had gone too far, and to rid his good-nature of a load, hunted up Thomas and made ample apology."[17] Thereafter, Lincoln did not omit satiric barbs so much as temper them with more nuanced self-satire that highlighted his character as a self-made man.

"Splendidly successful charges": Lincoln on Military Heroism

During and after the U.S.-Mexico War, then–U.S. Representative Lincoln played politics by deflating notions of military heroism through sometimes raucous self-satire. For example, in a July 27, 1848, speech, Lincoln mocked his own war record as a captain in the Black Hawk War and then attacked that of U.S. Senator Lewis Cass, Democratic presidential nominee and hero of the War of 1812. Lincoln's prefatory self-satire displayed to his auditors his self-effacing good humor and prevented the possibility of similar charges being levied against him. Lincoln's tactic was to cast aspersions upon Cass's military record by demeaning his own, thus bringing Cass down to his (self-satirized) level through the comparison.

> By the way, Mr. Speaker, did you know I am a military hero? Yes sir; in the days of the Black Hawk war, I fought, bled, and came away. Speaking of Gen: Cass' career, reminds me of my own. . . . It is quite certain I did not break my sword, for I had none to break; but I bent a musket pretty badly on one occasion. If Cass broke his sword, the idea is, he broke it in de[s]peration; I bent my musket by accident. If Gen: Cass went in advance of me in picking huckleberries [whortle-berries], I guess I surpassed him in charges upon the wild onions. If

he saw any live, fighting indians, it was more than I did; but I had a good many bloody struggles with the mosquetoes; and, although I never fainted from loss of blood, I can truly say I was often very hungry. Mr. Speaker, if I should ever conclude to doff whatever our democratic friends may suppose there is of black cockade federalism about me, and thereupon, they shall take me up as their candidate for the Presidency, I protest they shall not make fun of me, as they have of Gen: Cass, by attempting to write me into a military hero.[18]

Lincoln here was responding to a Democratic campaign strategy that emphasized Cass's 1812 war record in an attempt to counter Whig candidate General Zachary Taylor's advantage as a more recent and more famous war hero. Cass's biographer notes, "Veterans were trotted out at every crossroads to greet the 'brave old volunteer' and he was hailed as the 'Father of the West.'" To respond, Lincoln, at the time an unknown first-term congressman, engaged in satiric leveling by portraying his own military exploits as silly, undignified, and useless and then making repeated comparisons between his experiences and those of Cass. Satiric leveling challenges presumed hierarchies of value through invidious comparisons between high and low, spiritual and material, serious and the ludicrous. Lincoln, in equating his own demeaned experiences to Cass's alleged heroism, tainted Cass by mere insinuations of connections to Lincoln. He conflated high and low, hero and fool, noble officer and marauding hick. Just as important, Lincoln's verbal satire exposed the rhetorical techniques used to "write" Cass "into a military hero"; in doing so, Lincoln called into question not just Cass's heroism but any use of heroism for political ends, an admittedly tenuous approach in a year in which the Whigs nominated Taylor, especially since later in his speech, Lincoln went on to laud Taylor in glowing terms as "par excellence, the hero of the Mexican war."[19]

Lincoln's joke that he would be taken up as a "candidate for the Presidency" echoed those of Crockett, who in his autobiographies consistently, and somewhat ludicrously, hinted at being coerced into accepting "the presidential chair." Crockett's autobiography reveals a similar penchant for self-mockery and for "telling good humoured stories" on the campaign trail.[20] Lincoln's joke also carries an unintentional irony, because when he was president, his critics did "make fun of" him by belittling his abilities as commander in chief through reference to his service in the Black Hawk War. For example, in the satiric campaign biography *The Only Authentic Life of Abraham Lincoln* (1864), the anonymous writer shifts from grandiloquent to deflating language to describe Lincoln's service: "The ghastly battle-field now saw his towering form stalk, gloomy, magnificent and tremendous, through the thick vapors of the cannon's mouth. At least such would have been the case, had it not been for the Indians who resolutely refused to come near Abraham's regiment." This joke, however, does not go nearly as far as Lincoln's own description of his experiences in his speech against Cass. The pamphlet *The Lincoln Catechism, Wherein the Eccentricities and Beauties of Despotism Are Fully Set Forth: A Guide to the Presidential Election of 1864* (1864) told a similar joke but in the question-and-answer format of a catechism, thus structuring Lincoln barbs with question as setup and answer as punch line.

> *VII.*
> Was Mr. Lincoln ever distinguished as a military officer?
> He was—In the Black Hawk war.
>
> *VIII.*
> What high military position did he hold in that war?
> He was a cook.
>
> *IX.*
> Was he distinguished for anything except for his genius as a cook?
> Yes—he often pretended to see Indians in the woods, where it was
>   afterwards proved that none existed.
>
> *X.*
> Was he ever in any battle?
> No—he prudently skedaddled, and went home at the approach of the
>   first engagement.[21]

Of course, Lincoln was not a cook in the Black Hawk War but, rather, the elected captain of his volunteer company and is not known to have turned tail in battle.

These authors, then, resorted to libel in their mockery of Lincoln, who had already mocked his own service in much the same manner as both satires. Lincoln himself consistently painted his military exploits in a decidedly unheroic and folly filled light. Even in his own 1860 campaign biography, Lincoln downplayed his military heroism. After noting of his election as captain of his company that "he has not since had any success in life which gave him so much satisfaction," Lincoln described his service in particularly banal terms, disposing of it in a single sentence: "He went to the campaign, served near three months, met the ordinary hardships of such an expedition, but was in no battle." He actually saw a bit more action than his 1860 campaign autobiography claims. After enlisting for a third term of service, he helped bury five men killed by Native American warriors.[22] Even so, derogating symbols of heroism yielded distinct political dividends for Lincoln. In depicting himself as decidedly unheroic, he seemed to demean himself, but in light of his attack on heroism, he presented himself and the associated symbology of the nonmilitaristic, self-made man as reasonable alternative to the cult of military heroism.

Lincoln's willingness to mock himself allowed him to carve out rhetorical space from which to mock others. This is apparent in the speech against Cass, which Lincoln began by seeking to answer Georgia's Alfred Iverson's charges that "we [Whigs] have deserted all our principles, and taken shelter under Gen: Taylor's military coat-tail." Instead of defending Taylor as a politician, Lincoln ceded that military hero worship might not be the best political strategy and instead attacked Democrats for their own consistent recourse to it. "[C]an he," Lincoln asked about Iverson, "remember no other military coat tail under which a certain other party have been sheltering for near a quarter of a century? Has he no acquaintance with the ample military coat tail of Gen: Jackson?" Lincoln adopted a harsher tone after claiming that the military "coat tail was used, not only for Gen: Jackson himself; but has been clung to, with the gripe [*sic*] of death, by every democratic candidate since."

> Like a horde of hungry ticks you have stuck to the tail of the Hermitage lion to the end of his life; and you are still sticking to it, and drawing a loathsome sustenance from it, after he is dead. A fellow once advertised that he had made a discovery by which he could make a new man out of an old one, and have enough of the stuff left to make a little yellow dog. Just such a discovery has Gen: Jackson's popularity been to you. You not only twice made President of him out of it, but you have had enough of the stuff left, to make Presidents of several comparatively small men since; and it is your chief reliance now to make still another.[23]

Lincoln used Jackson's august reputation to condemn subsequent Democratic presidents as "comparatively small men" and animalized them as

　　　　　　　　　　　　　　　　　　"Little Big Man"

"dogs." Additionally, as he did throughout his political career, Lincoln here repurposed an apolitical joke for political satire.

Lincoln proceeded to parody political biography, noting that in trying to tie a "military tail" to Cass, his supporters and his biographers were "like so many mischievous boys tying a dog to a bladder of beans. True, the material they have is very limited; but they drive at it, might and main." Lincoln also used wordplay to refigure heroism as a descriptor of cowardice and graft. First, he joked that Cass "*in*vaded Canada without resistance, and he *out*vaded it without pursuit," rendering ridiculous military notions of invasion and retreat.[24] He moved to the more serious matter of insinuating that General Cass has been guilty of defrauding the federal government. In 1838 Cass had been accused of misappropriating $63,000 of public money for personal use while serving as superintendent of Indian Affairs. Though he was exonerated after a congressional investigation, Whigs revived graft rumors in 1848, claiming that "if his loot was loaded into wagons, the train would reach from Detroit to Toledo."[25] Lincoln's version of this accusation punned on military language, building up Cass as a "General of splendidly successful *charges*," only to deflate him with an allegation: "charges, to be sure, not upon the public enemy, but upon the public Treasury." Lincoln then trotted out facts and figures of Cass's salary and expenses, claiming that he received pay for "doing service, and incurring expenses, at several different *places*, and in several different *capacities* in the *same* place, all at the same *time*." Lincoln defended himself from the repercussions of his allegations by expressing mock reverence and awe.

> I have introduced Gen: Cass' accounts here chiefly to show the wonderful physical capacities of the man. They show that he not only did the labor of several men at the same *time*; but that he often did it at several *places*, many hundreds of miles apart, at the same time. And at eating, too, his capacities are shown to be quite as wonderful. . . . Mr. Speaker, we have all heard of the animal standing in doubt between two stacks of hay, and starving to death. The like of that would never happen to Gen: Cass; place the stacks a thousand miles apart, he would stand stock still midway between them, and eat them both at once; and the green grass along the line would be apt to suffer some too at the same time. By all means, make him President, gentlemen. He will feed you bounteously,—if—if there is any left after he shall have helped himself.[26]

This sarcastic account of the "wonderful physical capacities of the man" demeaned Cass through charges of graft (not to mention "fat" jokes) and mocked hero worship via a tongue-in-cheek performance of it. Throughout the speech, by fashioning his own symbols, Lincoln revealed the mechanics of how symbols of heroism are politically constructed. Comparative formulations, such as "I bent my musket pretty badly on one occasion . . . by accident," "I guess I surpassed him in charges upon wild onions," and "I had a good many struggles with the mosquetoes," all undermined the mythmaking process by repopulating it with ludicrous content that smeared Lincoln, Cass by comparative association, and "heroism" as a valid political qualification.

Lincoln defended this verbal abuse as a purely defensive tactic: "I repeat, I would not introduce this mode of discussion here; but I wish gentlemen on the other side to understand, that the use of degrading figures is a game at which they may not find themselves able to take all the winnings."[27] Of course, this was a game that Lincoln was very fond of playing, even as he averred that he was forced to play it. The comic effect of Lincoln's physicality as he spoke rendered these concepts all the more ludicrous, based on accounts of Lincoln's time in the House of Representatives. Other House members are said to have laughed "at the way he would stride down the aisles as he spoke, coat-tails flying." "[T]he speech was pretty good," Ohio Congressman William "Sausage" Sawyer commented, "but I hope he won't charge mileage on his travels while delivering it." Lincoln's speech only added to his reputation as the House's top wag whose witty stories won him friends throughout the Capitol.[28]

This was not the sole instance of Lincoln's rhetorical abuse of Cass that year. Throughout a speaking tour in New England, Lincoln continued to pillory the Democratic presidential candidate. Lincoln described his tour thusly: "with hayseed in my hair I went to Massachusetts, the most cultured State in the Union, to take a few lessons in deportment." As Lincoln learned eastern manners, New Englanders imbibed his western idiom. Whig leader Henry J. Gardner, who would later become governor of Massachusetts, remembered Lincoln's "style and manner of speaking," which "were novelties in the East," on display in a speech in Worcester on September 12, 1848. According to Gardner, "his sarcasm of Cass, Van Buren and the Democratic party was inimitable, and whenever he attempted to stop, the shouts of 'Go on! go on!' were deafening." Lincoln spoke three days later at a Boston Whig club, and the *Boston Atlas* gave a favorable review:

"Little Big Man"

"for sound reasoning, cogent argument and keen satire, we have seldom heard equalled." In a newspaper account of Lincoln's speech at Taunton, Massachusetts, that same month, Dr. William Gordon, while vehemently opposing the political content of Lincoln's speech, stressed the comic effects that Lincoln achieved through his body and voice: "The speaker was far inferior as a reasoner to others who hold the same views, but then he was more unscrupulous, more facetious and with his sneers he mixed up a good deal of humor. His awkward gesticulations, the ludicrous management of his voice and the comical expression of his countenance, all conspired to make his hearers laugh at the mere anticipation of the joke before it appeared."[29] Despite the fact that these accounts disagreed on the quality of Lincoln's logic, their emphasis on his delivery of crowd-pleasing humor highlights the importance of the parodic to Lincoln's political performance.

During the 1852 presidential campaign, Lincoln again found himself in the now familiar position of demeaning the military service of a Democratic candidate, this time Franklin Pierce, and military service, in general, as a qualification for elected office while promoting a U.S.-Mexico War general, this time Winfield Scott, for the presidency. In a speech to the Springfield (Illinois) Scott Club, Lincoln responded to charges Stephen A. Douglas made against Scott. Lincoln noted that Douglas, in his speech, "runs a tilt at Gen. Scott as a military politician, commencing with the interrogatory 'Why has the whig party forgotten with an oblivion so complete all that it once said about military politicians?' I retort the question, and ask, why has the *democratic* party forgotten with an oblivion so complete all that *it* once said about military politicians?" Here, much like in his 1848 response on the House floor to a similar Democratic barb, Lincoln did not deny Douglas's charge; he merely reversed it to sanction his own ensuing burlesque. In the speech that followed, Lincoln accused Democrats of employing the very tactic of demeaning military service that he had used so comically in 1848 and, indeed, continued to use in this very speech. Lincoln went on to paint as "ludicrous" a biographical scene intended to depict Pierce's heroism and arrived at the sarcastic conclusion that Pierce supporters had "a pertinacious purpose to 'pile up' the ridiculous. This explains the new plan or system of tactics adopted by the democracy. It is to ridicule and burlesque the whole military character out of credit; and this [thus?] to kill Gen. Scott with vexation." He cited as an example of this strategy "how our own 'militia trainings' have been 'laughed to death' by fantastic parades and caricatures upon them." In painting a verbal picture of such a militia parade and then transferring that ridicule to Pierce, Lincoln kept the tone light while engaging more forcefully in the tactic of travestying military service, which he had, of course, just pilloried Democrats for doing. He milked such scenes for comic and political effect while laying the responsibility for disrespectful rhetoric at the feet of his political opponents. Burlesques of militia drills had long been a favorite trope of southwestern humor, from Oliver Prince's 1807 "Militia Drill" to Augustus Longstreet's 1835 *Georgia Scenes* to William Tappan Thompson's third Major Jones letter.[30] Lincoln's auditors' familiarity with such travesties allowed him to identify Pierce as a comic character in Lincoln's own update of the traditional militia sketch. Through such satiric deflection, Lincoln questioned the political usefulness of military heroism without the attendant devaluing of the experience of the Whig generals whose candidacies he sought to support.

Satiric Flattery in the Lincoln-Douglas Debates

In his famous 1858 senatorial campaign debates with Douglas, Lincoln consistently used satiric modesty to differentiate himself from his more renowned opponent, playing off Douglas's fame and his own relative political insignificance to ingratiate himself with his hearers. These audiences—both in person and through print—were certainly large. In addition to the huge crowds that attended the debates, coverage by shorthand reporters, wire services, and magazines, such as *Harper's*, ensured a national audience. When Lincoln collected his and Douglas's speeches in book form as *Political Debates*, it sold thirty thousand copies within a few months.[31]

Lincoln's use of false modesty in the 1858 debates was merely a continuation of a tactic that he had been deploying against Douglas for years. As early as 1852, in his Springfield Scott Club speech, Lincoln noted his and Douglas's shared political history and juxtaposed U.S. Senator Douglas's status as a rising star in the Democratic Party to the shortcomings of his own political career as a one-time congressman. He said, "I was reminded of old times—of the times when Judge Douglas was not so much greater man than all the rest of us, as he now is." In attaching to Douglas the sarcastic honorific of "Judge," Lincoln called attention to how Douglas had attained that title as a result of his self-serving drive to expand the Illinois Supreme Court. In this way, Lincoln—certainly, not for the last time—simultaneously praised and mocked Douglas, in this case by giving him a title that his audience would see as unjustified or tainted. Upon resuming his speech at the club's next meeting, Lincoln again started by building up Douglas, this time in apologizing to the audience for taking as his text a Douglas speech, having learned that a previous speaker discoursed on the same subject. In his mock apology, Lincoln claimed, "I dislike the appearance of unfairness of two attacking one. After all, however, as the Judge is a giant, and Edwards [Ninian W. Edwards, the previous Whig speaker] and I are but common mortals, it may not be very unfair." In this instance, Lincoln purported to take literally Douglas's nickname, "the little giant," a moniker that Douglas had already held for almost twenty years, in order to justify attacking him. Later in this speech, Lincoln recurred to this literalization of Douglas's nickname in leveling a charge that Douglas had been miscalculating or misrepresenting government expenditures in his attacks on Whigs. After questioning Douglas's numbers, Lincoln deadpanned, "Judge Douglas is only mistaken about twenty five millions of dollars—a mere trifle for a giant!"[32] Having earlier set up Douglas as an actual giant, Lincoln used understatement in jokes about scale in order to question Douglas's integrity. Lincoln began both sections of this speech by rhetorically raising Douglas to an elevated position and then spent the rest of his speech undercutting the basis for that elevation.

In an October 16, 1854, Peoria, Illinois, speech against the Nebraska Act, Lincoln continued this approach. He announced that he would respond at seven o'clock to a speech that Douglas had given, thus offering the audience a chance to eat dinner and return. In explaining that Douglas would then have an hour to reply to his speech, Lincoln joked that his motives for agreeing to allow "one of his high reputation and known ability" to rebut his remarks were "not wholly unselfish; for I suspected if it were understood, that the Judge was entirely done, you democrats would leave, and not hear me; but by giving him the close, I felt confident you would stay for the fun of hearing him skin me."[33] In this instance Lincoln deprecated his own abilities in order to display his good humor to his hearers, presenting himself as human, approachable, and appropriately deferential. Additionally, by offering himself as a target—a sacrifice to be skinned—Lincoln lowered the audience's expectations of his speech. He situated himself as an entertaining antithesis instead of as a debate-worthy equal. But in doing so he also drew attention to himself (in this case, literally by convincing the audience to stay) in a novel and engaging way.

From this position of ostensible inferiority, Lincoln used his embellished flattery of Douglas to tear him down. As Lincoln had previously done with the concept and symbols of heroism in his attack on Cass, he consistently described Douglas as a "great man" and then redefined "greatness" negatively. In this way Lincoln used Douglas's fame against him, specifically by lauding Douglas's prominence and then implying that one could not sustain such a position without compromising his principles. In an 1856 speech in Kalamazoo, Michigan, for example, Lincoln quipped, "Douglas is a great man—at keeping from answering questions he don't want to answer."[34]

By 1858 Lincoln developed his redefinition of greatness into a full-blown campaign strategy. For instance, in accepting the Republican nomination to run against Douglas for a U.S. Senate seat, Lincoln in his House Divided speech on June 16, 1858, rallied the audience against Douglas and his Kansas-Nebraska Act at the Republican state convention: "They remind us that *he* is a very *great man*, and that the largest of *us* are very small ones. Let this be granted. But 'a *living dog* is better than a *dead lion.*' Judge Douglas, if not a *dead* lion *for this work*, is at least a *caged* and *toothless* one."[35] Lincoln made it others ("they") who called Douglas a great man and then transformed that greatness into a position of impotence (*"caged* and *toothless"* lion) inferior to the position of the "small" men and *"living dog"* Republicans.

In addressing a more politically heterogeneous group at their July 16, 1858, debate in Springfield, Lincoln himself (instead of a distanced and othering "they") contrasted Douglas's greatness to Lincoln's own obscurity so as to juxtapose the political sycophantism of Democratic politics and the ethics of the Republican campaign and its candidate. Lincoln claimed, "Senator Douglas is of world wide renown. All the anxious politicians of his party, or who have been of his party for years past, have been looking upon him as certainly, at no distant day, to be the President of the United States. They have seen in his round, jolly, fruitful face, postoffices, land-offices, marshalships, and cabinet appointments, chargeships and foreign missions, bursting and sprouting out in wonderful exuberance ready to be laid hold of by their greedy hands. [*Great laughter.*]" Aside from the verbal caricature of Douglas's visage, this formulation does not expressly attack Douglas but rather the hangers-on that, Lincoln implies, necessarily come along with such fame, experience, and expectations of further achievements. Lincoln then provided an antithetical portrait of his own political circumstances: "On the contrary nobody has ever expected me to be President. In my poor, lean, lank, face, nobody has ever seen that any cabbages were sprouting out. [*Tremendous cheering and laughter.*]" Lincoln self-effacingly invoked the difference between his "poor, lean, lank, face" and Douglas's "round" face—to Lincoln's own advantage, of course. Lacking pedigree and pageantry, Lincoln and the Republicans could claim that they had "to fight this battle upon principle, and upon principle alone."[36] Through satire that targeted Douglas, Douglas's followers, and himself, Lincoln succeeded in portraying himself and his party as righteous underdogs battling the well-oiled machinery of purely political and, thus, necessarily amoral power.

Lincoln used a similar rhetorical ploy in the Ottawa, Illinois, debate on August 21, 1858, where he lamented the fact that Douglas had questioned Lincoln's truthfulness in implying a conspiracy between Douglas's popular sovereignty legislation and the U.S. Supreme Court's *Dred Scott* ruling. Lincoln first pretended to be flattered with some complimentary language Douglas had used to describe him even after he had leveled his conspiracy charge in an earlier debate. Referring to "my friend, Judge Douglas," Lincoln noted that Douglas "complimented me as being a 'kind, amiable, and intelligent gentleman.' . . . Then, as the Judge had complimented me with these pleasant titles, (I must confess to my weakness,) I was a little 'taken,' [*laughter*] for it came from a great man. I was not very much accustomed to flattery, and it came the sweeter to me. I was rather like the Hoosier, with the gingerbread, when he said he reckoned he loved it better than any other man, and got less of it. [*Roars of laughter.*]" Here Lincoln once again juxtaposed, through a folksy simile, Douglas as a "great man" to himself as a star-struck fan starved for the famous man's "flattery." He used this juxtaposition to set up a claim of Douglas's disingenuousness: "As the judge had so flattered me, I could not make up my mind that he meant to deal unfairly with me." But, of course, Lincoln told the crowd, he was mistaken. From here he built toward an angrier tone: "It is fortunate for me that I can keep as good-humored as I do, when the Judge acknowledges that he has been trying to make a question of veracity with me. I know the Judge is a great man, while I am only a small man, but *I feel that I have got him.* [*Tremendous cheering.*] I demur to that plea."[37] The audience, of course, recognized the humor of Lincoln's visual irony in presenting himself as a "small man" and Douglas as a "great man," since the discrepancy between their heights—Lincoln was a foot taller—would be readily and ludicrously apparent when they appeared onstage together. But Lincoln also contrasted Douglas's greatness to his own seeming insignificance to claim the justness of his cause. In spite of Douglas's fame, Lincoln had "got him" and now "demur[red]" not to Douglas but to his own charge and its justification. In this speech and others, Lincoln's constant references to Douglas's "greatness" offered modest deference to Douglas's reputation while questioning the basis of that reputation and of the worth of "greatness" as incarnated in Douglas.

This satiric treatment of Douglas's "superiority" was not limited to oral debate. Lincoln also parodied the political theater of Douglas's arrivals at the debates, which was full of over-the-top pomp and circumstance. For example, Douglas traveled to the Ottawa grounds in a horse-drawn carriage, with an attendant band, supporters waving banners, and cannons booming. Lincoln, who deplored such pageantry, mocked it heavily. Of Douglas's cannons, he had said previously, "There is a passage, I think, in the Book of the Koran, which reads: 'To him that bloweth not his own horn—to such a man it is forever decreed that . . . his horn shall not be blowe-ed!'" At another time he fiddled with a harmonica and claimed that was his band. And, most publicly, he rode to the Freeport, Illinois, debate, August 27, 1858, in a covered wagon in a burlesque of the pageantry of Douglas's arrival in a coach. An offended Douglas, seeing this display, insisted on walking to the debate.[38]

In both his verbal and visual satires of Douglas, then, Lincoln took advantage of the multivalence of status symbols by reversing their affective associations. Lincoln successfully turned the emblems of prestige, greatness, and accomplishment against Douglas's deployment of them as his qualifications for office. Lincoln built Douglas up as "great" and then undermined reverence for greatness while demeaning himself as a "dog" or a "small man" with a "poor, lank, lean face" but imbued those descriptions with a populism that appealed to his audiences and mapped to prevailing myths of the self-made man. In his senatorial campaign against Douglas, Lincoln's humble self-fashioning sanctioned his good-humored jokes and stories, allowing him to present himself as a man of the people in contradistinction to the more professional and prestigious Douglas. The press, anyway, seemed to appreciate this approach. The *St. Louis Missouri Democrat* praised Lincoln on September 30, 1858, for treating "his opponent with a deference which the latter is incapable of reciprocating." As Douglas himself complained in an interview, "Every one of his stories seems like a whack upon my back. . . . Nothing else—not any of his arguments or any of his replies to my questions—disturbs me. But when he begins to tell a story, I feel that I am to be overmatched."[39] By pretending himself to be "overmatched," Lincoln could "overmatch" Douglas.

In an 1878 *Scribner's Monthly* piece, Noah Brooks remembered Lincoln's approach: "He admitted away his whole case, apparently, and yet, as his political opponents complained, he usually carried conviction with him." Brooks also recalled "once meeting a choleric old Democrat striding away from an open-air meeting where Lincoln was speaking, striking the earth with his cane as he stumped along and exclaiming, 'He's a danger-ous man, sir! a d——d dangerous man! Makes you believe what he says, in spite of yourself!'" This angry confession is a testament to the affective power of Lincoln's rhetoric: in carefully crafting his homespun image as an honest but fallible rustic, Lincoln through his self-presentation assured his audiences that his power was truly representative, of the people instead of above them. Bray observes what he calls "the paradox of satire" in "the democratic logos of antebellum western America," which is "that it both levels and distinguishes individuals. In the name of the people demagogues must be 'taken down,' yet 'the people' demand that only the best, the most accomplished logicians, speak in their name."[40] The trick for Lincoln was to convince the people that he was not attempting to replace a demagogue like Douglas but to more fully "speak in their name." He accomplished this in his self-satiric utterances by negating the positive content of symbols of heroism and greatness while attaching positive political connotations to oppositional symbols of simplicity, modesty, and rusticity.

Winning by Losing: Strategic Modesty as Presidential Tactic

Once elected to the presidency, Lincoln, though famously still enjoying a good joke, used less-satiric rhetoric in public discourse and did not engage heavily in attack politics in his official speeches. Part of this, of course, has very much to do with the dignity of the office as well as with Lincoln's attempt to unite the country during the Civil War. The solemnity of most occasions for his speeches often precluded the use of humor and vitriol. In proclaiming a national fast day, for example, Lincoln did not crack jokes or insult the South (though his political enemies certainly implied that he did). Lincoln as president was hardly able to engage in "little big man" political rhetoric; coming from the holder of the highest elected office in the country, such tactics would come off as disingenuous at best, weak or desperate at worst. Tactics, after all, are the "art of the weak" precisely because "power is bound by its very visibility."[41]

Even though Lincoln stood at the apex of political power as President of the United States, he still managed to engage in tactics somewhat anal-ogous to the "little big man" strategy by abjuring authority in order to win by losing. Two examples of behind-the-scenes political maneuvering are Lincoln's handling of the Fort Sumter crisis in 1861 and of Secretary of Treasury Salmon P. Chase's presidential ambitions. One of the first pieces of business on Lincoln's desk as president was a March 5, 1861, note informing him that troops stationed at Fort Sumter in the Charleston harbor were running low on supplies and would have to give up the fort or starve within six weeks. Lincoln did not surrender the fort to, and, thus, recognize the power of, the Confederacy, as this would create a public-opinion disaster demoralizing to Northern morale. Nor did he forcefully resupply the fort with food, arms, and reinforcements, a move that would offend not-yet-seceded Border States and some Northerners who demanded that the government avoid involving itself in acts of forceful coercion of seceded states. Rather, Lincoln chose the middle ground. He informed South Carolina governor Francis Wilkinson Pickens that he would attempt to peacefully resupply the fort with provisions only.

The maneuver allowed Lincoln to refigure the weakness of his position into a strength in the public's eye, reprovisioning the fort nonviolently forced the Confederacy's hand while insulating the federal government from charges of coercion or aggression. In this way, Lincoln "cast coercion in the mold of defense," outsmarting his opponents and shielding his administration from blame or responsibility for starting a war.[42] Tellingly, Lincoln and his cohorts described the fall of Sumter to each other in the terms of "winning by losing." Lincoln told friend and adviser Orville Browning that the fort, in falling, "did more service than it otherwise could"; Bostonian Oliver Ellsworth described the loss of Sumter as "the greatest victory the people ever realised; it has done its work *effectually*."[43] As these language choices show, Lincoln's administrative tactics were quite similar to his self-satiric political and campaign strategies. During the Fort Sumter crisis, Lincoln let everything go except the main chance; in forcing the South to live up to its own grandiloquent rhetoric, he redefined the seceded states as the aggressor instead of a victim of federal strength.

Though the stakes and nature of the problem differed, Lincoln used a similar strategy in response to Chase's underhanded seeking of the Republican nomination in 1864 while still serving as Lincoln's secretary of treasury. In this case, as with Fort Sumter, Lincoln turned a seemingly negative situation to his own strategic advantage. Though friends advised Lincoln to accept Chase's resignation or at least to forbid him from such political maneuvering, Lincoln said that he would prefer to let "Chase have his own way in these sneaking tricks than getting into a snarl with him

"Little Big Man"

by refusing him what he asks." This deference was not mere politeness or timidity. Rather, he understood that Chase would be less of a threat if he kept busy with his cabinet duties than if he were free to launch a presidential campaign. Additionally, Lincoln was well aware that Chase's presidential ambitions would make him work harder to be seen as an effective and distinguished treasury secretary. This ploy is evident in a joke attributed to Lincoln wherein he responds to calls to remove Chase with a "little story."

> That reminds me of a farmer out West. He was ploughing with his old mare Nance one hot summer day, and his son was following another plough in an adjoining furrow. A horse-fly got on Nance's nose, and the son kept yelling to his daddy to stop and get the fly off the mare's nose. The father paid no attention to his vociferous son for a while. Finally the son kept yelling about the fly on Nance's nose until the old man answered,—
>
> "Now, low-a-here, jist keep quiet; that ere fly on Nance's nose makes her go faster."

Like most Lincoln stories, this one turns humor into satire by repurposing an apolitical joke to specifically political purposes, as an allegory to simplify a complex political situation. In this case, Chase's ambitions to replace Lincoln are rendered as a benefit to Lincoln's administration; the "horsefly" of ambition spurs Chase to go about his work with greater energy. To keep Chase in his cabinet, Lincoln killed his treasury secretary's presidential bid with kindness. In one of Chase's many letters complaining about Lincoln's "disjointed method of administration," he admitted that "the President has always treated me with such personal kindness and has always manifested such fairness and integrity of purpose, that I have not found myself free to throw up my trust. . . . So I still work on."[44] Here as elsewhere, Lincoln used his opponent's strength against him by appealing to his vanity and ambition. In his dealings with Chase and in the Fort Sumter crisis, Lincoln redefined the terms of engagement to his own advantage. Such nuanced statesmanship belies his aw-shucks demeanor and humble background and, thus, underscores the synergy Lincoln saw among modesty, political rhetoric, and political practice.

CHAPTER 3

The Rail-Splitter
President

"So you're Abe Lincoln?"

"That's my name, sir," answered Mr. Lincoln.

"They say you're a self-made man," said the Democrat.

"Well, yes," said Mr. Lincoln, "what there is of me is self-made."

"Well, all I've got to say," observed the old man after a careful survey of the statesman before him, "is, that it was a d——n bad job."

This story, purported to be an exchange between Lincoln and an old Illinois Democrat after Lincoln had been chosen as the state's Republican candidate for president in 1860, demeans Lincoln's awkward appearance (but, then, so did Lincoln) while reinforcing his success story.[1] Taking his physical appearance as representing the quality of his rise in the world, the joke mocks Lincoln as the ultimate embodiment of the self-made man. Self-made men personify the ideals (and, as the above joke shows, the paradoxes) of representative democracy. That is, if elected officials are supposed to be somehow of the electorate but superior, to stand for our ideals and interests but also to work in a national instead of local milieu, then we need politicians who can move comfortably between Washington, D.C., and places like rural Illinois and translate them to each other. Lincoln's satire and his personal history helped him to assure voters and politicians that he could do precisely this. The concept of representation also implies that the representative is not just a stand-in for his or her constituents but also a model for them. Through the nascent antebellum rhetoric of the self-made man, Lincoln fostered an image of himself as representative in this way. He was deeply invested in this rhetoric, which, at midcentury, "represented a heroic ideal," and he consciously crafted an identity and narrative to fit it. Indeed, historian Richard Hofstadter, in characterizing the "myth of the self-made man," contends, "Keenly aware of his role as the exemplar of the self-made man, he played the part with an intense and poignant consistency that gives his performance the quality of a high art."[2]

This manufactured identity that mapped to the familiar rags-to-riches storyline began with Benjamin Franklin's own self-fashioning in his *Autobiography* and reached its apotheosis in the person of Abraham Lincoln, the backwoodsman-turned-president.[3] Lincoln's rise coincided with the era of the self-made man in American culture. Beginning in the 1830s, a spate of novels, self-help books, and conduct manuals narrated paths to economic and moral success through hard work and self-culture. Such overlaying of individual and national progress mirrored Lincoln's story and his politics. Lincoln labored to perpetuate his folksy image, which emphasized both his connection to common people and his impressive, lifelong efforts at self-improvement. Lincoln highlighted the very fact of his self-making by foregrounding both his current position and his humble origins, a move that celebrated his rise while mitigating satiric attempts to paint him as a backwoods rube. Analysis of Lincoln's and his campaigns' use of the rhetoric and politics of the emergent concept of the self-made man reveals how visual satires that ridiculed Lincoln's humble origins ultimately backfired, instead making him appear *more* representative of Americans rather than *less* qualified for office.

The Politics of Self-Making

The story of Lincoln's rise was made famous not only by mythologizers, such as Horatio Alger, but also by Lincoln himself. For instance, in an 1832 handbill in which he first offered himself as a candidate for the Illinois General Assembly, Lincoln announced, "I was born and have ever remained in the most humble walks of life. I have no wealthy or popular relations to recommend me. My case is thrown exclusively upon the independent voters of this county, and if elected they will have conferred a favor upon me, for which I shall be unremitting in my labors to compensate."[4] In this speech the twenty-two-year-old Lincoln highlighted his solitary condition: he lacked wealthy and influential benefactors, and leaving home to strike out on one's own was an important element of the myth of the self-made man. He then described the political work he wished to do as "labors," connecting farming and manual labor to the political process in a concrete way.

Lincoln certainly shaped his life narrative to conform to the rhetoric of the self-made man, who, in general, tended "to boast of his achievement, to exaggerate the obscurity of his origin."[5] Lincoln *was* born in a log cabin and *did* rise from tremendous poverty, but he seems to have exaggerated his penchant for physical labor. Indeed, in his early years, Lincoln was considered almost indolent. Neighbor John Romine remembered that Lincoln in his Indiana days "was awful lazy: he worked for me—was always reading & thinking—used to get mad at him." Lincoln's cousin Dennis Hanks, too, thought that "Lincoln was lazy—a very lazy man—He was always reading—scribbling—writing—Ciphering—writing Poetry &c.&c." Lawyer Stephen T. Logan thought Lincoln, upon his arrival in Springfield, to be "sort of a loafer." Lincoln's own stepmother said he "didn't like physical labor—was diligent for Knowledge—wished to Know."[6] Lincoln's childhood preference for headwork over physical labor was not appreciated in a time and place when and where thinking was not yet fully embraced as actual labor. He came of age in a transitional historical moment when Americans were just beginning to redefine what constituted work, distinguishing mental and physical labor, and finally accepting both as real work.[7] So, in playing up in later years the very labor he seems to have loathed, Lincoln stressed his familiarity with both types of work and implied their permeability: that is, one could begin, out of necessity, with hard work and then self-educate oneself into headwork. He was careful to valorize labor while self-fashioning himself as a representative of those who could move beyond it. It seems that the further Lincoln got from his humble roots, the more he emphasized them.

For instance, Lincoln had a hand in the public relations blitz of self-made–man imagery that anchored his 1860 campaign. Illinois Republican politico Richard J. Oglesby, not Lincoln, came up with the famous "rail-splitter" and "Honest Abe" nicknames, but there is evidence that Lincoln understood the benefits of such symbols and approved, even encouraged, their use. The rail-splitter tactic—following in a well-hewn political tradition that stretches back through Andrew Jackson's "Old Hickory" image, William Henry Harrison's log-cabin campaign, and Zachary Taylor's "Rough and Ready" persona—was certainly effective; one Lincoln scholar calls the designation of Lincoln as a rail-splitter "the greatest publicity stunt ever staged for a political candidate." It functioned by aligning to the standard narrative of self-making in that it "made much more of where he had begun life than where he had ended up."[8]

Lincoln's previous mentions in political speeches of his laboring past, in part, sanctioned the rail-splitter symbol. In the 1860 campaign biography that he composed in the third person for attorney and journalist John Scripps, Lincoln described in detail his early poverty, his work as a laborer, surveyor, and merchant, and his various attempts to keep "soul and body together." He also included references to rail-splitting. Of his childhood, he said, "A. though very young, was large of his age, and had an axe put into his hands at once; and from that till within his twentythird [sic] year, he was almost constantly handling that most useful instrument—less, of course, in plowing and harvesting seasons." In this sentence Lincoln pictured himself as "constantly handling" the ax—a symbol of both labor and national progress—put down only to begin the equally important nation-building work of agricultural labor. He described his family's emigration to Illinois: "Here they built a log-cabin, into which they removed, and made sufficient of rails to fence ten acres of ground, fenced and broke the ground, and raised a crop of sow[n] corn upon it the same year. These are, or are supposed to be, the rails about which so much is being said just now, though they are far from being the first, or only rails ever made by A."[9] Lincoln here acknowledges and authenticates the mania for the "Lincoln rails" started at the Chicago convention, associates them with the self-sufficiency of western yeomanry, and, in assuring readers that he had split many another rail, situates the rails as emblematic of continuing labor instead of a one-time effort. Nearly two-thirds of this biography, which was written explicitly for a political campaign, narrates the struggles of Lincoln's prepolitical life, a striking proportion that indicates Lincoln's awareness of the political value of his origin story.

William Dean Howells's 1860 campaign biography *The Life of Abraham Lincoln* also structures Lincoln's story through tropes of the self-made man. Because Lincoln corrected a facsimile of this biography, we can assume that he at least tacitly agreed with its approach. In narrating Lincoln's youth, Howells stresses his "decent poverty" and an education that came mostly through "the rough and wholesome experiences of border life," through which Lincoln "ripened into a hardy physical manhood, and acquired a wide and thorough intelligence, without the aid of schools or preceptors."

In describing Lincoln's hardscrabble youth and cobbled-together education on the frontier as ultimately healthful, Howells resituates difficult circumstances as valuable opportunities for self-making. His description of Lincoln's use of the ax mirrors Lincoln's own verbiage: "Abraham was a hardy boy, large for his years, and with his ax did manful service in clearing the land. Indeed, with that implement, he literally hewed out his path to manhood; for, until he was twenty-three, the ax was seldom out of his hand, except in intervals of labor, or when it was exchanged for the plow, the hoe, or the sickle."[10] Other than a few rhetorical flourishes, this sentence repeats Lincoln's own description of his ax work (quoted above), with the important exception that Howells makes crystal clear the importance of the ax as a symbol of self-making in the wording "he literally hewed out his path to manhood" through "that implement." In Howells's political hagiography, the ax was not just a tool of national progress but also of individual improvement.

For Howells, Lincoln's supposed aptitude for labor is a metaphor for his governing style. Howells describes Lincoln's travel to sessions of the Illinois legislature in the terms of a striving youth making sacrifices for betterment of self and state: "Lincoln used to perform his journeys between New Salem and the seat of government on foot, though the remaining eight of the Long-Nine traveled on horseback." In the copy that he reviewed, Lincoln crossed out this passage and wrote in the margin, "No harm, if true; but, in fact, not true." This comment demonstrates Lincoln's awareness of the usefulness of such fictions, especially since the correction was to be implemented only in future editions published after the 1860 election. Howells used similar rhetoric in describing Lincoln's political approach in Congress: "as Abraham Lincoln never sat astride of any fence, unless in his rail-splitting days; as water was never carried on both of his square shoulders; . . . so, throughout his Congressional career, you find him the bold advocate of the principles which he believed to be right. He never dodged a vote. He never minced matters with his opponents."[11] The implication here is that his work as a laborer gave Lincoln a practical bent that made him less likely to equivocate politically.

Of course, the mythos of self-making had been deployed by politicians before Lincoln. It was Lincoln's political idol, Henry Clay, who coined the term "self-made man" in 1832, ten years before the epithet would be applied to Lincoln himself.[12] Previous generations of Lincoln's fellow Whigs had worked to associate ideas of national progress through internal improvements with the individual ethos of self-improvement. Many have noted the similarities between the 1860 Lincoln campaign's use of the rail-splitter image and Harrison's 1840 "log cabin and hard cider" campaign. But Lincoln, unlike the Virginia aristocrat Harrison, really did split rails and did emerge from poverty. A closer predecessor to Lincoln in terms of the political value of rustic self-presentation might be Tennessee congressman David Crockett.

Like Jackson before him and Lincoln after him, Crockett was a westerner, a veteran of the Indian wars, and a minimally formally educated, self-made man. Crockett was initially elected to Congress as a Jacksonian Democrat but split with Jackson over the issues of internal improvements and Western Tennessee land grants. After this split, Crockett liked to say that he was still a Jacksonian but that Jackson was not. According to the ghostwritten *Account of Col. Crockett's Tour to the North and Down East*, Crockett said,

> as long as General Jackson went strait [*sic*], I followed him; but when he began to go this way, and that way, and every way, I wouldn't go after him: like the boy whose master ordered him to plough across the field to the red cow. Well, *he* began to plough, and *she* began to walk; and he ploughed all forenoon after her. So when the master came, he swore at him for going so crooked. "Why, sir," said the boy, "you told me to plough to the red cow, and I kept after her, but she always kept moving."[13]

This joke prefigures Lincoln's use of humor as political allegory in its repurposing of a farming anecdote to attack Jackson as politically shifty. Its rusticity is highlighted by the northeastern context—a dinner party in Massachusetts—in which Crockett allegedly told the joke, again foregrounding his frontier roots.

After his political switch, the Whigs exploited Crockett—who, his biographers say, was politically naive—and refashioned him into a living legend and political attack dog. The basis of those attacks was Crockett's own back story as a legendary frontiersman. In his 1834 autobiography, Crockett described his origins in a manner similar to how Lincoln would characterize his own twenty-six years later. Crockett highlighted his modest beginnings: "I stood no chance to become great in any other way than by accident. As my father was very poor, and living as he did *far back in the back woods*, he had neither the means nor the opportunity to give me, or any of the rest of his children, any learning." Crockett claimed that his schooling only totaled about one hundred days. This parallels Lincoln's description of settling "in an unbroken forest," which limited him to attending "A.B.C. schools by littles" such that "the agregate [*sic*] of all his schooling did not amount to one year."[14]

Crockett's biographer in *Sketches and Eccentricities of Col. David Crockett, of West Tennessee* (1833) also situates Crockett within the nascent discourse of the self-made man. As does Howells in his biography of Lincoln, Crockett's author, pseudonym James F. Strange, seeks to present Crockett as simultaneously singular (as the title "Eccentricities" suggests) and exemplary, a model and representative of what was possible in America under Whig policy. To give one brief example of this tension, Strange describes Crockett, "A hunter, poor, entirely without education, and without family influence, he was called upon by a large majority of the citizens of his district to represent them . . . without one single advantage other than the mere gifts of nature. He had to contend with men of genius, of fortune, and refined education . . . [and yet] Colonel Crockett rose to distinction."[15] This formulation calls attention to Crockett's ability to beat the odds and achieve greatness but also, paradoxically, to his very ordinariness (which Crockett himself pointed to when he characterized his rise as due to "accident").

From this rhetorical position of the self-made frontiersman, Crockett, throughout his political career, engaged in comparative biography, juxtaposing his own rustic circumstances and practical experiences to what he portrayed as his opponents' luxurious ease. In his early career, for instance, running for the Tennessee legislature against Dr. William E. Butler, Crockett described his frontier roots and then blasted Butler as an aristocrat living a decadent city life. When he visited Butler's home, Crockett reportedly refused to walk on an expensive rug and told the story of it in subsequent speeches: "Fellow citizens, my aristocratic competitor has a fine carpet, and every day he *walks* on truck finer than any gowns your wife or your daughters, in all their lives, ever *wore!*"[16] This tactic is reminiscent of Lincoln's visual and verbal invective upon Illinois politicians, such as Usher F. Linder, George Forquer, and Stephen A. Douglas. These attacks functioned through a comparison between a self-made man with connections to the people and aristocratic politicians whom Crockett and Lincoln depicted as considering themselves to be above their constituents. Both Whig politicians consistently presented themselves as honest, hardworking, commonsense rustics (like their audience members) in comparison to their opponents, whom they painted as opportunistic, aristocratic political operators.

The Rail-Splitter President

Just how much of this Lincoln borrowed from Crockett's example is unclear. Though Crockett's biographies do not appear in Bray's bibliography of books that Lincoln likely read, Lincoln was certainly familiar with Crockett's political career and the mythology surrounding him. In any case, Lincoln's fellow congressmen saw the connection. As they had done with Crockett, representatives who served with Lincoln thought of him as a "comical wild and wooly westerner," "laughed at his awkward way of walking and the way he walked to the boardinghouse carrying books in a bandana handkerchief tied to the end of a pole. But by New Years [sic] they treasured him as 'the champion story-teller in the Capitol.'" As P. M. Zall relates, "because of the way he performed in debate and the way he looked and talked, congressional Whigs felt they had been blessed with another Davy Crockett."[17]

The Rail-Splitter President in Political Cartoons

A key difference between Crockett's heyday in the 1830s and Lincoln's in 1860 is the emergence of illustrated news. This newly pervasive medium allowed for the widespread dissemination of images of Lincoln, many of which portrayed him as he portrayed himself—as a laborer-turned-politician—thus further solidifying his status as a self-made man and visually connecting him to Northern voters.

A series of technological innovations in printing—including steam engines, rotary presses, new paper-making techniques, widespread use of lithography, and modernized processes for wood engraving—had advanced far enough by 1860 that, for the first time, voters could see political candidates' images in newspapers and magazines. First, the use of steam to power presses increased the speed of presses by the 1840s. Second, the widespread adoption of rotary presses, which used curved plates rather than flat surfaces to print, and stereotyped casting, which created the plates, meant that newspapers and magazines could be printed at far-faster speeds. Third, the shift from handmade to machine-made paper in the first half of the nineteenth century improved both the quality and quantity of newsprint. Fourth, the newly widespread use of lithography, invented in the 1790s, allowed for greater tonal variation. Many pictorial satirists worked in the medium of lithography in their newspapers and periodical satires and separately printed posters.[18]

Maybe most important for the rise of illustrated news was the increasing use at midcentury of wood engraving, which allows art and text to appear, relatively inexpensively, on the same page. As opposed to the old woodblock cut with woodworking tools that hammer an image into the wood, the newer wood engravings, made with a burin, which can move smoothly along a wood surface, were more-precise drawings. With the use of stereotyped printing plates, printers could lock up the relief images engraved in wood and cast them as part of a single plate, which saved wear and tear on the original relief block during printing.

These advances saved time and increased circulation of printed images. Lithography and wood-engraving processes allowed larger press runs and helped make it possible for newspapers and magazines to disseminate an image within two to three days of receiving the original drawing. *Frank Leslie's Illustrated Newspaper*, for instance, routinized wood engraving by machining the preferred wood from trees with trunks too small for full-page engraving into standard blocks of two square inches and bolting the blocks together to form a smooth block of any size. The head engraver drew the image's outline on this large block, which was then unbolted, and individual blocks given to engravers with specialized skills (for example, faces or background details) to complete. This division of labor further sped up the engraving process.[19]

All of these technological advances led to a boom of illustrated newspapers, including P. T. Barnum's short-lived *Illustrated News* in 1853 (which eventually folded into *Gleason's Pictorial Drawing-Room Companion*), *Frank Leslie's* (beginning in 1855), *New York Illustrated News* (1859–64), and *Harper's Weekly* and *Monthly*. These newspapers and magazines produced a "storehouse of images for the entire country, providing virtual presence for people otherwise remote from the drama of the polity." The use of illustrations helped to make news more exciting because the images broke up the monolithic page of print; by surrounding illustrations with elaborate borders to set them apart from the typeface, newspapers created "design conventions" that "likened news pictures to paintings in a gallery" and, thus, turned reading the news into a new experience. Photography existed, but there was not yet a method to reproduce photographs on the same sheet at the same time as print; therefore, cartoons reached many more people than did photographs. Graphic artists became important mediators, translating the world they reported on to the images of that world that readers consumed and internalized. When Lincoln first ran for president, political cartoons were newly omnipresent in the popular press. In speaking to a growing mass audience, cartoonists played a key role in shaping the public images

The Rail-Splitter President

of their caricatured subjects. The 1860 election was the first in which all candidates appeared visually in a wide array of illustrated newspapers and magazines containing a glut of political caricature. These caricatures and more-realistic portraits visually introduced voters to the presidential hopefuls and in doing so reinvented how American politics were presented to voters.[20]

Lincoln's consciously fostered image was ready-made for caricature; this historical fortuity mitigated the content of the cartoons and print satires lampooning him. His press savvy and practice as a satirist made him aware of the consensus-building power of combining satire with a homespun persona and, as a public figure, of how satire could be used against him. Lincoln's strategic use of his personal history and self-fashioning as a laboring man of the people helped him reap the benefits of American caricature without suffering (as much as other public figures, anyway) from its denigrations. Whereas satire and caricature usually undercut their targets' eminence, Lincoln cultivated a folksy *lack* of eminence as "Honest Abe" the "rail-splitter," a hardworking, self-made man of humble origins who maintained a distinct affinity with common Americans. Lincoln was simultaneously *more* caricature-able than his opponents because of his unusual physical presence and his laboring background, which he highlighted through his self-presentation, and *less* susceptible to the negative ramifications of such caricature because through that modest and satiric self-presentation, he inoculated himself more than most caricatured subjects from the potential for a loss of prestige. In this way, caricatures and satires of Lincoln seem to have played right into his hands.

Whereas pro-Lincoln political cartoons attempted to characterize him as a "common man uncommonly qualified to be president," anti-Lincoln images tried to paint him as an ungentlemanly lout. Cartoons depicting Lincoln negatively and cartoons depicting him positively relied upon the same visual shorthand, that is, emphasizing his height and homeliness, drawing him with an identifying ax, and/or depicting him as a jester or a laborer. As analysis of Lincoln cartoons shows, determining "which symbols the propagandist intends to be positive and which negative" does not necessarily signal whether these cartoons were actually read as absolutely positive or negative.[21] Some cartoons intending to associate negative symbolism with Lincoln actually depict him as a self-made man and not a backwoods boor, a charming humorist rather than a vulgar and inappropriate joker, a man of impressive stature instead of a grotesque giant. This is because Lincoln's self-satiric presentation anticipated these critiques and beat them to the punch, rendering them relatively innocuous. Lincoln, thus, crafted and controlled his image not only to win and maintain public support but also to shape criticism of him and exclude certain negative images. A laboring, joking, western man could not be dismissed as yet another East Coast elite or cunning operator, for example. Even some negative images of Lincoln safeguarded against potentially more-damaging criticisms.

In short, Lincoln, who has been called "the most visually conspicuous political figure in the history of the republic," actually benefited from the emergence of popular illustrated periodicals such as those listed above as well as in comic periodicals like *Vanity Fair, Frank Leslie's Budget of Fun, Funniest of Phun,* and *Phunny Phellow.*[22] Many cartoons echo Lincoln's campaign biography in depicting him as a laborer or farmer, using his identifying ax to physically go about political work. Harold Holzer, who has examined the Lincoln image extensively, points out that cartoonists and printmakers stressed "Lincolnian attributes that were physical, though decidedly civilian. In prints showing him as a railsplitter and flatboatman, Lincoln was portrayed as an American success story who escaped frontier poverty by sweat and strength. Even in caricature that mocked him, reminders of his strenuous life were much in evidence."[23] Holzer is right to notice the emphasis on physicality in Lincoln caricature, but he may underestimate the ideographic nature of caricature. In offering visual depictions of political activities, all cartoonists have to physicalize their subjects, that is, they need to draw objects instead of ideas in order to hit upon salient metaphors to convey their points. Since laborers deal more extensively with tactile objects than do politicians, Lincoln's self-identification and cultivation of his image as a laborer translated well to the medium of political cartoons, which work by materializing complex political issues into symbolic images. The symbols of labor, humor, and populism that Lincoln and his campaign referenced and behaviorally enacted offered caricaturists ready-made, positively tinted ideographs. For example, cartoonists could capture Lincoln's rail-splitter image in caricature through the easy-to-draw and easy-to-label symbols of the ax and the rail, which served as perfect physical symbols for the collected connotations Lincoln's supporters wished to disseminate in celebrating his self-making.

These depictions began with the 1860 general-election campaign. "The Tribune Offering the Chief Magistracy to the Western Cincinnatus" in the satirical magazine *Momus* on June 9, 1860, portrays *New York Tribune* editor and powerful Republican kingmaker Horace Greeley as beckoning to Lincoln to leave his farm work to take up the mantle of leadership in Washington (fig. 3.1). The cartoon's point is to insinuate that Greeley, identified by the word "TRIBUNE" on his coat, has the political power to court and appoint Lincoln as a presidential candidate. Indeed, Greeley's *Tribune* circulated widely in the Northern states and had about ten thousand readers in Illinois alone. More important is the image of Lincoln as a workingman, his sleeves rolled up to reveal his muscular arms, which wield his trademark ax. Lincoln here is a Cincinnatus, called from the fields to govern in a time of need. This trope—referring both to the Roman statesman Lucius Quinctius Cincinnatus, who quit his farm to serve Rome as dictator and resigned his office when his task was done, and to the U.S. Society of Cincinnati's celebration of Revolutionary War officers—was still trenchant in mid-nineteenth-century America. Specifically, political campaigns connected American agrarianism to political independence and, thus, celebrated their candidates' statuses as farmer-statesman, the "backbone of political democracy."[24]

In "The Last Rail Split by 'Honest Old Abe'" (fig. 3.2), another *Momus* cartoon from the 1860 campaign, Lincoln is pictured wielding a maul and using a wedge to split a rail, which is identified as the Democratic Party.

THE TRIBUNE OFFERING THE CHIEF MAGISTRACY TO THE WESTERN CINCINNATUS.

Figure 3.1. "The Tribune Offering the Chief Magistracy to the Western Cincinnatus." *Momus, June 9, 1860, 73. Courtesy, American Antiquarian Society.*

Figure 3.2. "The Last Rail Split by 'Honest Old Abe.'" Momus, *June 2, 1860, 61. Abraham Lincoln Presidential Library and Museum.*

The Last Rail Split by "¡Honest Old Abe."

Due in part to Douglas's disagreements with President James Buchanan, Democrats could not agree on a candidate at the 1860 Charleston, South Carolina, convention, and several delegates from the Deep South withdrew after their platform was rejected. Eventually, the party offered two separate candidates: John C. Breckinridge from Kentucky and Douglas from Illinois. In this cartoon, Lincoln's physical labor and his identification as the "rail" candidate become metaphors for political work, and the Lincoln-as-workingman image credits him with agency in effecting the split of his opposition party; he does it physically and emphatically.[25]

Such representations continued even after Lincoln took office. In the 1860 Currier and Ives poster cartoon "'Uncle Sam' Making New Arrangements" (fig. 3.3), the character of Uncle Sam (center, in knee breeches) stands before the White House, removing a notice that says, "Wanted. An honest upright and capable man to take charge of this house for four years. Undoubted testimonials will be required. Apply to Uncle Sam, on the Premises." He hands Lincoln notice reading, "I have hired [him] for four

The Rail-Splitter President

years from March 1st 1861." In this cartoon, Lincoln is pictured without a coat or vest, in suspenders and rolled-up shirtsleeves, and with his trademark ax. Such iconography is especially telling given the location—at the door of the White House—and the formality of dress of his unsuccessful opponents, John Bell, Breckinridge, and Douglas, who are waiting in line to make their respective cases to Uncle Sam. Lincoln's rusticity here differentiates him from the other candidates, all of whom look and speak in similar ways.[26]

Such depictions continued throughout Lincoln's tenure in office. *Harper's Weekly* was lukewarm toward Lincoln during the 1860 election because of the journal's extensive readership in the South as well as its moderation on slavery and other controversial issues, earning it the nickname "Harper's Weakly," but was generally supportive after the onset of the Civil War. *Harper's* "Lincoln's Last Warning," an October 11, 1862, Frank Bellew cartoon (fig. 3.4), again shows Lincoln in shirtsleeves wielding an ax. The tree is labeled "SLAVERY"; Lincoln tells a man, probably Jefferson Davis, "Now, if you don't come down, I'll cut the Tree *from under you.*" This cartoon renders Lincoln's composition of the Emancipation Proclamation as the physical labor of chopping down a

Figure 3.3. "'Uncle Sam' Making New Arrangements." Poster cartoon. *New York: Currier and Ives, 1860. Courtesy, American Antiquarian Society.*

LINCOLN'S LAST WARNING.
" Now, if you don't come down, I'll cut the Tree *from under you.*"

Figure 3.4. "Lincoln's Last Warning." *Frank Bellew,* Harper's Weekly, *October 11, 1862, 61. Courtesy, American Antiquarian Society.*

tree. Lincoln's physical prowess means that his "warning" is not an empty threat: he has the strength to complete the task.[27]

The Cincinnatus trope is another carryover from the election to Lincoln's term in office. For example, "Good Gracious, Abraham Lincoln!" from *Frank Leslie's Budget of Fun* in January 1861, tells the story of Lincoln's meeting with Columbia and the American eagle (fig. 3.5). Columbia, the American version of England's Britannia figure and dating from around 1800, was often drawn as she is here: beautiful, with long hair and a flowing gown, likely a nod to neoclassical American interest in Greek culture. But unique to this drawing is the apprehension that is obvious in Columbia's uneasy face and cowering posture upon seeing Lincoln's rough-and-ready appearance (he is still carrying the rails). In the caption, she asks Lincoln how he managed "to get the situation of overseer of my farm." Lincoln's election and the public's image of him (shaped both by the press and Lincoln himself) as simultaneously a rural worker and Western Cincinnatus had made possible this cartoon's imagination of the United States as a farm. Of course, if the republic is a farm, this version of Lincoln is presumably highly qualified to serve as "overseer." Lincoln's response in the caption shows him to be well-meaning but rough around the edges. He promises to "act on the squar" and work for "the interests of the hull farm." He will, he says, "take care that our blessed bird loses none of its pin feathers."[28]

Lincoln's emphasis of his laboring past led cartoonists to picture him doing other work besides that of an ax-wielding farmer. Often, this labor involved joining of some kind, a metaphor for Lincoln's attempts to save or reconstruct the national union. For example, in Joseph E. Baker's "The Rail Splitter at Work Repairing the Union," a July 1865 Currier and Ives

Figure 3.5. "Good Gracious, Abraham Lincoln!" Frank Leslie's Budget of Fun, *January 1861, 16. Courtesy, American Antiquarian Society.*

print, Lincoln uses his rail as a wedge to hold up the nation, represented as a ball, while vice presidential candidate Andrew Johnson uses needle and thread to sew the states back together (fig. 3.6). Johnson says to Lincoln, "Take it quietly Uncle Abe and I will draw it closer than ever!!" and Lincoln assures Johnson, "A few more stitches Andy and the good old Union will be mended!"[29] In "A Job for the New Cabinet Maker," which appeared in *Frank Leslie's Illustrated Newspaper* on February 2, 1861, Lincoln, again in work clothes and jacket-less, works as a cabinet maker, a pun on the president's role in selecting cabinet members to advise him (fig. 3.7). He dips a brush into a bucket of "Union Glue" and tries to paste together a gaping crack separating two pieces, one piece labeled "NORTH" and the other "SOUTH," of the cabinet on which he works.[30] Like other cartoons, this image concretizes into manual labor the abstract job of reuniting the nation. Associating Lincoln with his laboring past helped cartoonists nudge readers to view the process of reunification as simplified and, therefore, understandable and achievable.

"Cooperation," from the April 12, 1862, *Vanity Fair*, works in much the same way (fig. 3.8). The title is a pun on the occupation of "cooper," and the

Figure 3.6. "The Rail Splitter at Work Repairing the Union." Cartoon print. *Joseph E. Baker (New York: Currier and Ives, July 1865). Courtesy, American Antiquarian Society.*

The Rail-Splitter President

image depicts Lincoln as a cooper and the Union as a tub. With the help of an assistant in a dashing Zouave uniform (adapted from an elite battalion of French soldiers by various volunteer units from both the Union and the Confederacy), Lincoln engages in the tactile physical labor of saving the Union. His sleeves are again rolled up as he gets down to work.[31]

All of these examples picture political and military work as manual labor, thus offering Lincoln's working-class background as a fitting résumé for national challenges. These cartoons are remarkably similar in the ways in which they depict a hardworking Lincoln engaging in a manual-labor task that comes to represent his national political efforts. This derives, in part, from the ease of making physically representable actions of labor serve as visual shorthand for cartoonists. Lincoln's biography and self-presentation made the use of such shorthand entirely plausible and logical. Lincoln's image was a perfect fit with the emergent medium of political cartoons.

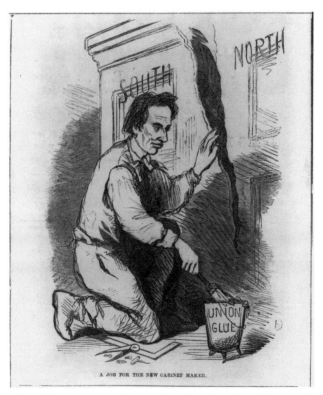

Figure 3.7. "A Job for the New Cabinet Maker." Frank Leslie's Illustrated Newspaper, *February 2, 1861, 5. Library of Congress.*

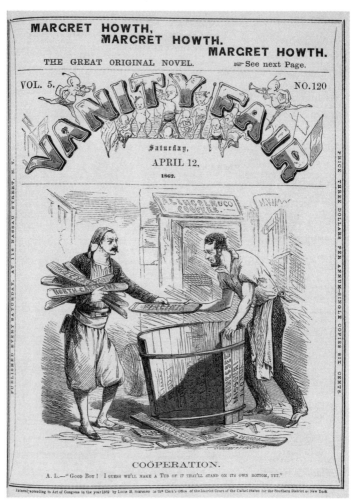

Figure 3.8. "Cooperation." Cartoon. Vanity Fair, *April 12, 1862, cover. Courtesy, American Antiquarian Society.*

The benefits of such images seem to have been self-sustaining. In an 1864 pamphlet, *A Workingman's Reasons for the Re-Election of Abraham Lincoln*, the anonymous author appeals to the (by this time) well-established notion that *"Abraham Lincoln is in the strictest sense of the phrase a man of the people."* In making this point, the author references popular images of Lincoln in circulation: "When you see him in the pictorials of the day with sleeves tucked up to his elbows, and axe in hand, or floating down some Western stream on a raft of lumber, it is no partisan fancy sketch designed to take the eye, and secure the votes of workingmen, but a simple reality of his early life. He has been placed in your circumstances. He has felt your necessities."[32] The author's reference to "pictorials of the day," presumably both serious portraits and satiric caricatures, hints at both their currency in popular culture and their influence on readers. In his eulogy of Lincoln, James Russell Lowell expresses similar sentiments in more elevated diction: "Homely, dispassionate, showing all the rough-edged process of his thought as it goes along, yet arriving at his conclusions with an honest kind of every-day logic, he is so eminently our representative man, that, when he speaks, it seems as if the people were listening to their own thinking aloud."[33] Both the pamphlet and Lowell's eulogy connect Lincoln's greatness to his representation of the common, working American people.

Harriet Beecher Stowe, famous author of *Uncle Tom's Cabin* (1852), the immensely popular and controversial novel written in response to the Fugitive Slave Law and credited with ratcheting up sectional tensions that led to secession and the Civil War, similarly eulogizes President Lincoln more in terms of his laboring past than his presidential greatness. Or, rather, like Lincoln, she promulgates the myth of the self-made man by figuring these two seemingly different subject positions, laborer and president, as appropriately united in the person of Lincoln. In her 1868 book *Men of Our Times, or Leading Patriots of the Day*, she claims, "Abraham Lincoln was in the strictest sense *a man of the working classes.* All his advantages and abilities were those of a man of the working classes, all his disadvantages and disabilities those of the working classes, and his position at the head of one of the most powerful nations of the earth was a sign to all who live by labor, that their day is coming. Lincoln was born to the inheritance of hard work, as truly as the poorest laborer's son that digs in our fields."[34] Stowe's brother Henry Ward Beecher, a clergyman, lecturer, and Lincoln supporter who served as an agent rallying support for the Union cause in Europe and was hired by the National Union Committee to speak in the final days of the 1864 campaign, was also one of the main forces behind the antebellum mythos of the self-made man. As such, Harriet Beecher Stowe certainly understood the power of the rhetoric that she deployed in this passage. For her, even Lincoln's faults were emblematic, class-based, and "American." After his death, then, Lincoln became even more central to the myth of self-making, as he came to represent not just a particular kind of frontier grit but, in a reunited country now without chattel slavery, a newly national sense of the ideal citizen as self-made.

The postbellum emphasis on the mythology of self-making can be seen on the July 8, 1865, cover of *Frank Leslie's Illustrated Newspaper* (fig. 3.9).[35] L. Hurz's drawing "Log Cabin Built by President Lincoln in Kentucky" is five years removed from the log-cabin campaign and a little over two months after Lincoln's death. Lincoln had lived in the White House for a little over four years, had achieved greatness, had put his poor Kentucky origins in the distant past, and had rewritten his life story from the "short and simple annals of the poor" to a narrative of diplomatic skill and ultimate self-sacrifice.[36] But in keeping his memory alive, the press increasingly harked back to his humble beginnings, thus cementing the legend of Lincoln that he himself helped to create.

LOG CABIN BUILT BY PRESIDENT LINCOLN IN KENTUCKY.—SKETCHED BY L. HURZ.

Figure 3.9. "Log Cabin Built by President Lincoln in Kentucky." *L. Hurz*, Frank Leslie's Illustrated Newspaper, *July 8, 1865, 1. Courtesy, American Antiquarian Society.*

The Rail-Splitter President

It seems, then, that Lincoln's real-life circumstances and political self-presentation influenced visual depictions of him and that, in turn, influenced the public by reminding them of his connection to the people and further instantiating his modest, self-satiric, homespun image. Lincoln's self-mocking stories and consciously humble biography provided a wealth of material for cartoonists to work with, and in this sense, Lincoln indirectly guided their treatments of him. The effect of the proliferation of "workingman" caricatures of Lincoln was to enhance further his homey, rail-splitter image and to inspire others' verbal and written depictions of him, which slightly altered Lincoln's image (in the case of *A Workingman's Reasons*, by pushing it further in the direction of mythology) and again inspired updated visual representations. In the new age of the illustrated newspaper, these cycles of visual images influencing textual depictions and vice versa became advantageously self-perpetuating.

CHAPTER 4

"Abraham Africanus the First": The Limits of Preemptive Self-Satire

---

The revilings which have been shouted from Richmond,—
the cries of "Ape," "Monster," "Imbecile,"—revilings
repeated by the low ministers of faction at the North,—are
but the ribaldry in which the offscourings of an aristocracy
based upon the denial of human rights display their hatred
of those principles of democracy of which Mr. Lincoln is the
worthy representative.

—*Charles Eliot Norton, 1865*

In his first American political cartoon, Thomas Nast captures the difference between Northern and Southern images of Lincoln during the secession crisis. The first panel of the drawing "President Lincoln's Inaugural" in the March 23, 1861, *New York Illustrated News* depicts the Northern take on Lincoln's inauguration: the president, gendered female in a dress, probably to evoke Eirene, the Greek goddess of peace, holds a palm branch in his right hand and scales of justice in his left, with the word "Peace" in the background (fig. 4.1). The second panel imagines the Southern reaction through the caption, "This is the way the South receives it"; Lincoln, teeth gritted and wearing Roman war garb, brandishes a sword and holds his foot atop his enemy, with the word "War" in the background.[1]

86

This is the way the North receives it.

THE PRESIDENT'S INAUGURAL,
And

This is the way the South receives it

Figure 4.1. "President Lincoln's Inaugural." *Thomas Nast, New York Illustrated News, March 23, 1861, 320. Courtesy, American Antiquarian Society.*

This image makes clear the limited sphere of influence for the ameliorating effects of the Lincoln image machine. The vicious pillory that Lincoln received in the Southern press, the English press, and the more vitriolic elements of the Northern Copperhead press is well documented. A media historian summarizes such treatment: "In the Copperhead papers, and some others, the President was referred to by such epithets as 'a slang-whanging stump speaker,' 'half-witted usurper,' 'mole-eyed,' 'the present turtle at the head of the government,' 'the head ghoul at Washington,' and other epithets even less complimentary. . . . He was accused of all kinds of misconduct—having drawn his salary in gold bars, drunkenness, granting pardons to get votes, needless slaughter of men for the sake of victories, even treason."[2]

If Lincoln used satiric modesty to fit into prevailing myths of the self-made man and, therefore, inoculate himself from criticisms dismissing him as a backwoods boor, such a tactic would be less effective for audiences that did not share in the lionization of the American Dream. The English held a different conception of class mobility; Southerners were culturally aligned with England and largely committed to an economic system that Lincoln and others saw as antithetical to self-making; and Northern sympathizers

"Abraham Africanus the First"   87

with the Southern cause were often tied to Southern society and economy and suspicious of American westerners.

Indeed, the myth of the self-made man was largely an American (and Northern) phenomenon. Four of the five conduct manuals studied in *The Self-Made Man in America: The Myth of Rags to Riches* were published in the North or East. Horatio Alger Jr., whose rags-to-riches narratives helped fuel the myth in the second half of the nineteenth century, characterizes Lincoln's rise as a particularly American phenomenon, in his biography *Abraham Lincoln, the Young Backwoods Boy, or How a Young Rail-Splitter Became President* (1883). He maintains, "In England the path of promotion is more difficult, and I doubt whether any one circumstanced as Abraham Lincoln was could ever have reached a commanding position." Though actual opportunities for social mobility among different nations are fairly equal, according to historian Irvin Wyllie, attitudes towards mobility vary greatly.

> The ideal of rising in [U.S.] society was never subjected to the continual and devastating criticism of exponents of a traditional ideal of culture as it was in England, where . . . the self-made man was one of the prime targets of such big guns as Carlyle, Ruskin, and Arnold. The contrast between nineteenth-century English and American attitudes toward self-improvement appeared often in the comments of English travelers in America. Mrs. Trollope [Frances Trollope, British author of the 1832 travel narrative *Domestic Manners of the Americans*], who visited American in the 1830's, was stupefied by the pride that leading Americans took in the fact that they were self-taught and self-made, which, as she acidly remarked, meant to her only that they were taught badly and badly made.[3]

Trollope's sarcastic diagnosis echoes the joke about Lincoln's self-making being a "d——n bad job." This intimates that what to Trollope and other European visitors was distasteful was to Northern Americans joke-worthy but laudable. Either way, groups of people—in the United States and abroad—who did not buy into the rhetoric of the self-made man were less likely to appreciate Lincoln's self-presentation (much less his politics); his self-aware, preemptive satire, therefore, did not mollify such groups.

Lincoln's supporters often saw his detractors as anathematic to self-making and, therefore, to American egalitarian principles. To give one example, author and critic Charles Eliot Norton opined in the *North American Review* at the close of the Civil War that

"Abraham Africanus the First"

one great source of the mis-esteem in which he is held by many persons in the community not opposed to him as partisans, and of the attacks upon him by the misnamed Democratic party of the present day, arises from the fact that there is a large class of Americans by birth or adoption, including the larger part of the spurious Democratic party, who are not Americans in principle. They have inherited prepossessions from the past; they belong to the old world of class-privilege, of inequality, of unjust political distinctions. They breathe with difficulty the free air of the new world. Their souls are not open to the inspiring and ennobling doctrines on which the future is to be builded fair.

Norton lumped together Northern Copperhead and Southern vitriol by describing it as initiated in Richmond and then "repeated" in the North by "low ministers of faction." He painted these detractors as decidedly un-American—either immigrants or "not Americans in principle" particularly in their continuing dedication to class stratification. Specifically, Norton claimed, those who opposed the war effort and Lincoln, whom he described as the paragon of American-ness, did so because as "the offscourings of an aristocracy based upon the denial of human rights," they clung to "the old world of class-privilege, of inequality." Such citizens would, of course, be unmoved by Lincoln's anti-aristocratic charms.[4]

An anatomy of common tropes in anti-Lincoln satires produced by Southerners, the pro-Southern, Copperhead press in the North, and English humor periodicals reveals limitations to the argument posited in chapter 3 about how Lincoln mitigated satiric treatments of him through his self-satiric performance of the self-made man. All this is *not* to say that the Northern press, as opposed to the British press and Southern press, portrayed Lincoln in a uniformly positive light. Rather, Northerners' investment in the concept of the self-made man allowed Lincoln some wiggle room for image amelioration through self-satiric self-fashioning in a way that attitudes in the South and in England did not abide or even recognize.

"Black Republican": Lincoln in the Southern and Copperhead Press

Before and even during the 1860 election, Southern vitriol focused less on Lincoln than on the Republican Party, in general. However, when the Civil War began, Southerners scapegoated Lincoln as the personification of Northern aggression; as a result, he bore the brunt of Southern calumny.

Throughout all media, including newspapers, magazines, speeches, songs, and pamphlets, Southerners labeled Lincoln as "a simpleton, a buffoon, a drunkard, a libertine, a physical coward, and a pornographic story-teller" as well as a "'tyrant,' a 'fiend,' and a 'monster.'" Depicting Lincoln as the personification of all that was "coarse, brutal, boorish, and crude among their foes," Southern treatments of Lincoln attempted to other him by mocking his humble origins (notably, in Kentucky) and deriding his rise to prominence.[5] For instance, former South Carolina Governor John Manning complained to his wife in 1860 that the Republicans had nominated "a wretched backwoodsman, who have [sic] cleverness indeed but no cultivation."[6] In seeking to puncture Lincoln's self-made–man image, many Southern and Copperhead satirists and caricaturists went beyond mocking him as an awkward everyman. Rather, many satiric depictions of Lincoln relied heavily on long-standing satiric tropes of target-as-Satan or target-as-racialized-other.

These satires of Lincoln commonly went to the extreme of labeling him as devilish or demoniac. "Masks and Faces," a woodcut image published in November 8, 1862, in the short-lived *Southern Illustrated News* (September 1862 to March 1865), shows Lincoln removing a face mask to reveal his true self, Satan (fig. 4.2). At his feet lies a scroll with the date of the Emancipation Proclamation, and the caption reads, "King Abraham before and after issuing the EXCLAMATION PROCLAMATION."[7] The implication of this unsubtle image is that the proclamation is a diabolical act preplanned by a diabolical author, who is not merely a tyrant, "King Abraham", but, worse, evil incarnate. Similarly, Baltimore artist Adalbert Johann Volck's engraving "Lincoln Signing the Emancipation Proclamation" depicts a devilish Lincoln with one foot atop the Constitution, and the pen with which he signs the proclamation is dipped in Satan's inkpot (fig. 4.3). The office decorations—a hooved desk, a statue in a hangman's mask, and a picture of the bloody slave revolt of St. Domingo, the 1791–1804 Haitian Revolution—associate diabolism with emancipation.[8]

Another Lincoln-as-Satan cartoon, "Abduction of the Yankee Goddess of Liberty," appeared in the November 14, 1863, *Southern Punch* (fig. 4.4). This illustrated comic newspaper, which began in August 1863 but died out in 1865, featured political cartoons, jokes, war news, and anecdotes and was consistently and virulently anti-Lincoln and anti-Union. In this cartoon Lincoln, described as the "Prince of Darkness," kidnaps the goddess of liberty and carries her to "his infernal regions." The goddess cries,

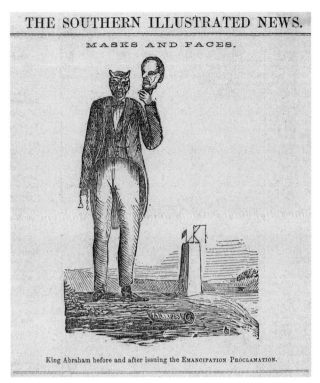

Figure 4.2. "Masks and Faces." Southern Illustrated News, *November 8, 1862, 8. Courtesy,* American Antiquarian Society.

Figure 4.3. "Lincoln Signing the Emancipation Proclamation." *Adalbert Johann Volck,* *engraving, October 1862. Courtesy, Lilly Library, Indiana University, Bloomington, Indiana.*

"Monster of Perdition, let me go!" Lincoln replies, "Never! You have been preaching about the Constitution too long already. I was the first to rebel against constituted authority. 'Hell is murky!' You go thither!"[9]

In each of these examples, a proclamation that Southerners saw as defying or undermining the U.S. Constitution is visually connected to Satan's rebellion against God's law. Such a claim was made from shaky legal grounds, since, in Lincoln's view, anyway, the secession that led to the war that eventually necessitated emancipation was itself unconstitutional.

Abduction of the Yankee Goddess of Liberty.
THE PRINCE OF DARKNESS (ABRAHAM LINCOLN) BEARS HER AWAY TO HIS INFERNAL REGIONS.

Goddess—Monster of Perdition, let me go !

Abraham—Never ! You have been preaching about the Constitution too long already. I was the first to rebel against constituted authority. "Hell is murky!" You go thither !

Figure 4.4. "Abduction of the Yankee Goddess of Liberty." Southern Punch, *November 14, 1863, 4. HarpWeek.*

"Abraham Africanus the First"

Describing Lincoln either as the devil or in league with the devil was also a common trope in satires attacking Lincoln in print. For example, the 1864 Copperhead satire *The Lincoln Catechism*, whose cover is figure 4.5, begins, "What is the Constitution?" "A compact with hell—now obsolete." "By whom hath the Constitution been made obsolete?" "By Abraham Africanus the first." This work cross-references another pamphlet also printed by New York publisher J. F. Feeks in 1864, *Abraham Africanus I* (fig. 4.6). That pamphlet begins with a dramatic poem in which Lincoln and Satan discuss the terms of their deal for Lincoln's soul. Lincoln reminds Satan that he had promised a "Monarchy, or at least a First Consulship." Other parts of the genre-shifting satire (it moves from dramatic monologue to prose narrative to framed burlesque biography) portray Lincoln as a hard drinker with "a general odor of liquor pervading him" (actually, he drank very rarely) and attempt to puncture Lincoln's self-made–man image through the fictional Lincoln's own testimony under the spell of a mesmerist. In this unconscious state, Lincoln disavows his humble heritage, claiming instead that he is of aristocratic descent, and admits that he only ever split one rail—"and that's the *rail* truth." *Abraham Africanus I*, thus, works not by reinhabiting or redeploying Lincoln's symbolic use of the self-made man but by denying the veracity of Lincoln's use of those symbols and the value of self-making, in general. In the narrative, the devil himself is embarrassed by Lincoln's uncouthness: when Lincoln attempts to tell him "a western story," which he describes as "a d——m good joke," Satan scolds, "Don't swear. . . . Forget your old habits for once, and behave yourself while in the presence of a gentleman *as* a gentleman." When Lincoln, while mesmerized, claims that he will not leave office if voted out in the 1864 election, Salmon P. Cheezey (a thinly disguised Salmon P. Chase) complains, "This comes of elevating such trash."[10] Here the pamphlet's self-contradictory class critique of Lincoln—that is, it both denies Lincoln's humble roots and excoriates them—is linked to his supposed diabolism. But, though the thin fictional device of the mesmerism narrative sanctions the pamphlet's slander of Lincoln, the setup and accusations are so outlandish that they would presumably not convince readers to change their preexisting attitudes towards Lincoln.

Artists have relied upon devils and allusions to Satan to represent evil throughout history. On one level, then, in the images and writings discussed above, the satirists deployed Satan and Satanism to imply that Lincoln's Emancipation Proclamation is an evil act. But satanic associations in images also attempt to create "objectifications of the shame that is wished or visited upon the figures portrayed."[11] Though these cartoons and print satires certainly could not make Lincoln feel shame for his actions, they did enact a symbolic moral judgment of those actions for their readers. But in reducing Lincoln to a symbol of evil, these satires and caricatures fail to engage with the materials of Lincoln's life, work, and looks. Rather, they scapegoat Lincoln as an inscrutable, supernatural actor for a policy with which they do not agree.

Another typical strategy of Confederate cartoonists and Copperhead satirists is to racialize Lincoln as a "Black Republican." Before Lincoln's inauguration, this charge was levied at all Republicans resisting the spread of slavery into new territories, instead of Lincoln, in particular. In the 1858 U.S. Senate campaign debates, Stephen A. Douglas had labeled Lincoln a "Black Republican" in an obvious race-baiting ploy. Lincoln was well aware of these criticisms and even addressed them directly in his Cooper Union speech in February 1860. In this speech, Lincoln, speaking directly

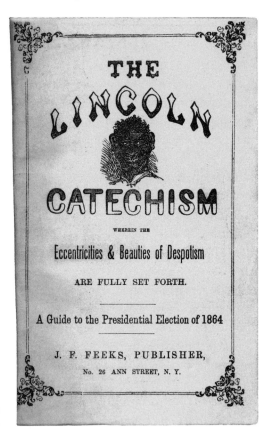

Figure 4.5. *The Lincoln Catechism.* Title page. *New York: Feeks, 1864. Courtesy, Lilly Library, Indiana University, Bloomington, Indiana.*

"Abraham Africanus the First"

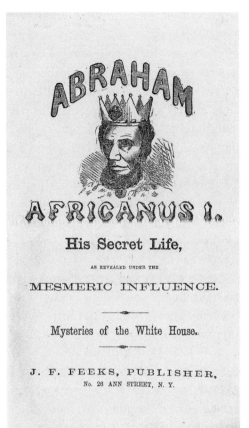

Figure 4.6. *Abraham Africanus I.*
Title page. *New York: Feeks, 1864.*
Abraham Lincoln Presidential Library
and Museum.

to "the Southern people," "if they would listen—as I suppose they will not," preemptively put epithets in their mouths: "[W]hen you speak of us Republicans, you do so only to denounce us as reptiles, or, at the best as, no better than outlaws. You will grant a hearing to pirates or murderers, but nothing like it to 'Black Republicans.' In all your contentions with one another, each of you deems an unconditional condemnation of 'Black Republicanism' as the first thing to be attended to. Indeed, such condemnation of us seems to be an indispensable prerequisite—license, so to speak—among you to be admitted or permitted to speak at all." With this address, Lincoln couched an attack on Southerners in the form of a complaint against their unfair attacks on Republicans. This allowed him to engage in ridicule while claiming to be above the fray, even as he mocked Southern speech by referring to popular sovereignty as "the 'gur-reat pur-rinciple.'"[12] He could do so with more freedom because before receiving the Republican nomination, he was not yet the party's standard bearer and, therefore, not its symbolic embodiment.

But once thrust into the national spotlight, Lincoln came to be seen as the personification of "Black Republicanism," and Southerners and Copperheads responded with satires that attacked more through racist paranoia than wit or policy critique. Even physical descriptions of Lincoln in Southern newspapers and magazines tend to racialize him as black. For instance, in 1860 the *Charleston (SC) Mercury* described Lincoln as follows: "A horrid looking wretch he is, sooty and scoundrelly in aspect, a cross between the nutmeg dealer, the horse swapper, and the night man, a creature 'fit evidently for petty treason, small strategems and all sorts of spoils.' He is a lank-sided Yankee of the uncomliest visage, and of the dirtiest complexion. Faugh! after him what decent white man would be President?"[13] In this passage, Lincoln's homeliness is given a racial cast. As the examples above yoke together a class-based critique of Lincoln as a lout with charges of diabolism, so, too, did depictions of Lincoln that insinuated blackness ("sooty," "dirtiest complexion") combine with markers of lower-class status ("a cross between the nutmeg dealer, the horse swapper, and the night man").

Some treatments of Lincoln as a "Black Republican" were fairly innocuous. The Andrew Adderup joke book *Lincolniana, or the Humors of Uncle Abe* (1864), published by Feeks, begins with the story "An Involuntary Black Republican," about a mischievous boyhood Lincoln who plays a trick wherein an ink bottle pours on his schoolmaster, "deluging the bald head in a shower of Stygian blackness" (fig. 4.7). "Lincoln" in the joke labels the incident as "the first *black* Republican ever made in Kentuck." The joke pivots mostly on a depoliticizing pun that redefines the "making" of "black Republicans" as a literal darkening process through ink, though it does touch on Lincoln's storytelling and hints at fears of amalgamation, especially in the punch line, where Lincoln says that "the conversion was too sudden" because the schoolmaster "afterwards married a widow and——twelve negroes."[14]

Most satires on Lincoln that relied on race-baiting were, of course, more rancorous. Southwestern humorists, for, example, mocked Lincoln's appearance to excoriate his racial attitudes. Both George Washington Harris's "Sut Lovingood" and Charles H. Smith's "Bill Arp" characters were semi-literate backwoods rubes, who, in their newspaper epistles, addressed Lincoln as one of their own. In a series of pieces in the *Nashville (TN)*

"Abraham Africanus the First"

FIRST BLACK REPUBLICAN MADE IN OLD KAINTUCK.

"I stood just outside of the door expecting the result; he sat down and then leaned back. Down came the bottle, deluging the bald head in a shower of Stygian blackness."

Figure 4.7. "First Black Republican Made in Old Kaintuck." *Andrew Adderup*, Lincoln-iana, or the Humors of Uncle Abe *(New York: Feeks, 1864). Abraham Lincoln Presidential Library and Museum.*

Union and American between February 28 and March 5, 1861, Harris un-folds a narrative in which Sut helps Lincoln evade assassins on his trip to Washington, D.C., for the presidential inaugural. Sut describes Lincoln, "Ove all the durned skeery lookin ole cusses fur a president ever I seed, he am decidedly the durndest. He looks like a yaller ladder with half the rungs knocked out." Again, Lincoln is described as exceedingly ugly and as "yaller" vaguely racialized. When Sut, trying to save Lincoln from murderers, asks if Lincoln understands "southern law," Lincoln responds, "Only es it tetches niggers." Lincoln later tells Sut, "You wer right tu tell him [a stranger Sut had been talking with] that I warn't smart, ur I woudent be here in sich imedjut danger, jis fur my party an a pack ove durned niggers."[15] By rendering Lincoln's speech through Sut's dialect, Harris already makes it appear that Lincoln "warn't smart" and through the content of their exchange connects that stupidity to a political obsession with "durned niggers." In this way Harris uses southwestern humor, to which Lincoln often had recourse in political situations, against him. In fact, Harris's strategy of demeaning Lincoln by bringing him down to Sut's social and intellectual level mirrors the "little big man" tactic that Lincoln used throughout his political career.

Similar use of southwestern humor to damn Lincoln for his racial politics can be seen in Smith's creation Bill Arp, whose "letters to Lincoln" were published in the Rome, Georgia, paper *Southern Confederacy* in April 1861, January 1862, and December 1862. Smith, like Harris, was a staunch Rebel, and his Arp letters were popular with Southern readers. One scholar of Southern humor says that Smith's writing "was to the South what Artemus Ward's was to the North." Like Harris's Sut, Smith's Arp treats Lincoln as an equal and as a fellow humorist, but he has a bone to pick with Lincoln over the threat of emancipation. The month before the Emancipation Proclamation was to take effect, Arp wrote to Lincoln that the time

hastens on to that eventual period which you have fixed when Africa is to be unshackled, when Niggerdom is to feel the power of your proclamation, when Uncle Tom is to change his base and evacuate his cabin, when all the emblems of darkness are to rush frantically forth into the arms of their deliverers, and with perfumed and scented gratitude embrace your Excellency and Madam Harriet Beecher Stowe! What a glorious day that is to be! What a sublime era in history! What a proud culmination and consummation and coruscation of your political hopes! After a few thousand have clasped you in their ebony arms it will be a fitting time, Mr. Lincoln, for you to lay yourself down and die. Human ambition can have no higher monument to climb. After such a work you might complete the immortal heroism of your character, by leaping from the topmost pinnacle to your glory upon the earth below.

"Abraham Africanus the First"

Arp here amuses his readers by coyly urging Lincoln to commit suicide in celebration of emancipation. As in several other satires on Lincoln, Harriet Beecher Stowe, author of *Uncle Tom's Cabin*, is figured as Lincoln's abolitionist right-hand woman and, in the royal metaphor, his wife. This passage, which oozes sarcasm, equates emancipation with miscegenation (i.e., "rush frantically forth into the arms of their deliverers," "clasped you in their ebony arms") and fears of a black takeover of the United States ("Africa is to be unshackled"). Of course, Lincoln had addressed such connections himself in a humorous fashion at a Chicago speech during his 1858 senatorial campaign: "I protest, now and forever, against that counterfeit logic which presumes that because I do not want a negro woman for a slave, I do necessarily want her for a wife. [10] In making this tasteless, crowd-pleasing joke, Lincoln anticipated and preemptively defused the logic of emancipation as amalgamation that would be used against him in subsequent years.

The 1862 print satire *God Bless Abraham Lincoln: A Solemn Discourse by a Local Preacher* also tried to damn Lincoln and his cohorts by playing to its audience's racial fears. In response, like Arp's letter, to Lincoln's Emancipation Proclamation, the pamphlet's sustained irony offers "praise" of Lincoln for his "great work": that of "changing the Black Moor, African, or Negro, vulgarly called, into white men." According to the preacher, "laws to that effect have recently been ordained"; he ironically lauds "the practicability of turning the Blacks into Whites, and *vice versa* Whites into Blacks." In the odd, science-fiction-worthy scenario that follows, the preacher explains that white men will be killed and white women forced to procreate with black men.

All capable of bearing arms or matrimony are either to be slain by the edge of the sword or rendered unfit for service. This being the case, the White skin females marriageable or widowed will be innumerable. The Male Blacks or Ethiopians, having passed through the war unscathed, and well fed, must have allotted to each as many white females as Mrs. Harriet Beecher Stowe and the Strong-minded Women of the East, sitting in Faneuil Hall, as a Disposing Congress, of which Mrs. Stowe will be Speaker, may judge him competent to manage. Those of the white females who prove fastidious and who will not take to the Ethiopian Skins, are to be flung out, in Butler Fashion, for the use of the unbridled and unbroken-in Black Ourang-Outangs, to deal with them according to their natural instincts. At the same time, the Ethiopian females must be restrained, under penalty of death, from all intercourse with those of their own color. . . . They are to be assorted and classified; those found of proper age and health are to be reserved for white men.[17]

Like Arp's letter, this "sermon" sets up Lincoln and Stowe as the faces and agents of abolitionism. It, too, sarcastically lauds Lincoln and Stowe as the nation's primary emancipators, along with General Benjamin "Beast" Butler. Butler earned this nickname in 1862 for his ironhanded measures as military governor of New Orleans, where he also instituted a controversial emancipation policy. "Butler fashion" likely refers to his 1862 Order No. 28, which proclaimed that any woman of New Orleans found insulting a Union soldier or officer "shall be regarded and held liable to be treated as a woman of the town plying her avocation."[18] The pamphlet mirrors Arp's epistle in its fears of emancipation as miscegenation, described here as a legally enforced dictum of Lincoln's diabolical doings. The sermon moves on to imagine a litany of disastrous consequences of the Emancipation Proclamation: visions of a dystopia in which freed African Americans ravage the land, "Ships lie rotting at the wharves. . . . The Banks are closed and broken. . . . The Money Changers find their tables overthrown, and their occupation gone. . . . The Farmers find their Fields laid waste, Dwellings and Barns demolished." Indeed, the pamphlet concludes in a jeremiad against Lincoln as the abolitionist extraordinaire: "Finally, let Hell open wide its Jaws, and jubilant of the works of Abolitionism, belch forth flames and lightening, and, in derision of the Most High, *laugh out*—in Thunders that will shake the earth and startle the ear of Heaven—GOD BLESS ABRAHAM LINCOLN!"[19] This final summation joins the Lincoln-as-Satan trope with the "black Republican" trope to offer a fantastic conspiracy theory of an apocalyptic postemancipation nation.

The Lincoln Catechism offers a similarly paranoid vision of a racially amalgamated future in America. In advertising in the front and back matter for other Feeks publications, the pamphlet is advertised as *The Lincoln (Negro) Catechism*, highlighting its racial focus, and the pamphlet's cover features a caricature of a smiling African American. The contents of this fifty-page pamphlet are no less subtle.

IV.

What is a President?

A general agent for negroes.

"Abraham Africanus the First"

V.

What is Congress?

A body organized for the purpose of taxing the people to buy negroes, and to make laws to protect the President from being punished for his crimes.

VI.

What is an army?

A provost guard, to arrest white men, and set negroes free.

. . .

XV.

What is the meaning of the word "patriot?"

A man who loves his country less, and the negro more.

The pamphlet's title situates Lincoln as its subject and sets him up at the beginning through his title "Abraham Africanus the First," and the job description, "general agent for negroes," as behind the conspiracies elucidated thereafter. The catechism form allows the author to juxtapose banal questions (i.e., "What is a President?" "What is a Congress?" "What is an army?" "What is a loyal league?") with shocking answers that act as punch lines and through their consistent invocation of "negroes" drive home the pamphlet's paranoid point.

"Lesson the Third" in *The Lincoln Catechism* shifts to a parody of the Ten Commandments. The Ten Commandments of "loyal leaguers"—referring to clubs established during the war to promote the Union and support the war effort—include the following:

Thou shalt have no other God but the negro.

Thou shalt make an image of a negro, and place it on the Capitol as the type of the new American man.

Thou shalt swear that the negro shall be the equal of the white man. . . .

Thou mayest commit adultery—with the contraband.

Thou shalt steal—everything that belongeth to a slaveholder.

Here the invocation of biblical language, such as "Thou shalt" and "belongeth," is meant to make Lincoln's wartime actions appear blasphemous as well as unconstitutional, especially because most of the Ten Commandments are inverted to make biblical wrongs of Lincolnian rights (e.g., "Thou shalt make an image," "Thou shalt swear," "Thou mayest commit adultery," "Thou shalt steal").[20]

"Lesson the Ninth" asks,

"Does the Republican party intend to change the name of the United
  States?"
"It does."
"What do they intend to call it?"
"*New Africa.*"[21]

This reversal plays on Americans' postcolonial anxieties by imagining an
ascendant imperial power as itself the object of racial imperialism. It also
recalls *God Bless Abraham Lincoln*, which similarly relocates the center of
the American empire to "St. Domingo and Liberia."[22] But the ludicrousness
of the entelechy of "Lesson the Ninth"—that ending slavery will somehow
turn America into an African colony—denied it serious polemical value
with voters during election season. It was designed less to convince than
to stir up fear and resentment.

Southern visual caricatures of Lincoln were no more understated.
For example, a sketch from Richmond animalizes Lincoln in order to
associate him with a racial slur (fig. 4.8). Specifically, Lincoln is depicted
as a monkey—a common stereotype levied at African Americans—who
celebrates the Emancipation Proclamation with a tiny, dancing slave.
The racist paranoia that motivated these satires targets Lincoln as the
official incarnation of its fears, but the race-baiting that constitutes the
billingsgate in no way touches the actual Lincoln.[23] All of these attacks
on Lincoln operate through preposterous vitriol instead of critiques rooted
in Lincoln's actual policy, history, character, or even physical appearance;
as such, while they could certainly amuse or frighten Lincoln haters or
even readers desirous of a harmless laugh, they likely would not succeed
at reexamining the dominant Lincoln symbols or narrative in a new light.

The reach and effect of these cartoon and print satires in the 1860s
are unclear. Confederate caricatures were certainly much less plentiful
than their Northern counterparts. Volck, the pro-Confederacy artist most
discussed by modern scholars, is a case in point. He was forced into under-
ground distribution of his prints in small numbers, and his influence was,
thus, limited to a local audience of like-minded subscribers. His works likely
went unseen in the seceded states during the war and, as such, had little
to no effect on the Confederate war effort. So, while Volck is considered the
most recognizable of Confederate caricaturists today, his fame arose after
the war, due to a recovery of his works thirty years after the war ended.[24]

"Abraham Africanus the First"

Figure 4.8. Untitled drawing. Richmond, Virginia, January 14, 1863. *Courtesy, Lilly Library, Indiana University, Bloomington, Indiana.*

Material shortages also account for the Confederacy's paltry production and dissemination of cartoons and print satire during the Civil War. Much of the ink, paper, and machinery used for periodical production came from the North and was, therefore, unavailable; anyway, the majority of able-bodied artists and printmakers had been forced into military service. Most engravers and lithographers working in the publishing capitol of Richmond had to work almost entirely on official images instead of on satiric prints. In addition to a lack of equipment and manpower, many journals could not pay the exorbitant postage charged in the Confederacy. Partly for these reasons, "so called 'Confederate caricature' of Lincoln is a rare genre indeed."[25]

Harris's and Smith's southwestern humor did reach a wider audience through the distribution of newspapers like the *Nashville (TN) Union and American*, located in a loyal Border State, and the *Southern Confederacy*, published deep in Confederate territory, especially when one considers the nineteenth-century culture of reprinting. There is certainly evidence of the popularity and circulation of the Arp letters. One observer remembered in 1882 that Smith's Arp letters "were welcomed by a large circle of readers. During the war every solider in the field knew Bill Arp's last." A friend of Smith claimed in 1878, "I doubt if any papers ever produced a more thorough sensation than did the letters written by Major Smith during the war. It is true they had a certain local pungency that added zest and that pronounced sectional feeling inflamed their reception into a triumph." Due to the popularity of their backcountry characters, Harris and Smith may have influenced their readers to share those characters' views of Lincoln as a backwoods peer. However, such an association did not necessarily amount to a full denigration. This may be why these authors focused so insistently on their perceptions of Lincoln's racial politics. For his part, in collecting his wartime Arp letters in book form as *Bill Arp, So Called: A Side Show of the Southern Side of the War* (1866), Smith sought to recontextualize these letters not as pro-Southern propaganda but as a historical document "worthy of preservation, as illustrative of a part of the war—as a side-show to the Southern side of it—an index to our feelings and sentiments."[26]

The potential reach of Copperhead anti-Lincoln satires is more intriguing. The fact that Southern newspapers routinely borrowed and recirculated Northern satires on Lincoln shows that Copperhead satires may have had the very effects—demoralizing Northerners and giving hope and succor to Southerners—that Unionists feared.[27] Feeks's catalog, which includes *The Lincoln Catechism*, *Abraham Africanus I*, and *Lincolniana, or the Humors of Uncle Abe*, evinces the intentions and distribution strategies of one Copperhead publisher. According to the back matter of both *Lincolniana* and *The Lincoln Catechism*, these works were part of a series Presidential Campaign for 1864. Other titles listed and described include the following:

"Abraham Africanus the First"

Book First Prophet Stephen, Son of Douglas
And many marvellous things shall come to pass in the reign of Abraham Africanus I. 12mo. *Price 15 Cents*, post free.

Book Second Prophet Stephen, Son of Douglas
And the wrath of King Abraham shall be kindled against the people because they love the Constitution and the laws of their fathers. *Price 15 Cents*, post free.

. . .

Songs and Ballads of Freedom
Inspired by the Incidents and Scenes of this present war, being the finest collection of Songs ever published. 12mo. *Price 15 Cents*, post free. Any of the above, single copies, 15 cents, one dozen, $1.50; one hundred, $10.

Trial of Abraham Lincoln
By the great Statesmen of the Republic, a Counsel of the Past, Spirit of the Constitution on the Bench, ABRAHAM LINCOLN a Prisoner at the Bar, his own Counsel. Single copies, *10 Cents*, one dozen, $1; one hundred, $10.

The bottom of the page reads, "For sale by all Booksellers and Newsdealers. Democratic Clubs and Committees supplied on liberal terms."[28] Based on the series name, the titles and descriptions of the pamphlets, and their prices, these pieces were mass-printed and—costing between ten to fifteen cents, the same price range as the famously cheap dime novels of the 1860s—priced to move, excoriating Lincoln in hopes of influencing the 1864 presidential election. The discounts for bulk orders and the specifically mentioned price break for "Democratic Clubs and Committees" imply that the pamphlets were for dissemination at political gatherings as campaign fodder. Ridiculous and slanderous as the content was, these pamphlets may have achieved fairly wide distribution among Copperheads and helped to reaffirm the suspicions and fears of Northerners who already distrusted Lincoln and his war motives. But if Feeks wanted to appeal to immigrants and other Northern voters with a vested interest in the American myth of the self-made man, he could not print pamphlets that denigrated Lincoln's famous self-making. Instead he denied that self-making (for example, by claiming an aristocratic lineage for Lincoln in *Abraham Africanus I*) and resorted to race-baiting and satanic imagery in his pillory of Lincoln and other Republicans.

"Penitent Punch": Lincoln in British Caricature

The Mason and Slidell incident of 1861, in which the U.S. Navy seized from a British mail packet two Confederate commissioners bound for diplomatic postings in Europe, raised tensions between Britain and the United States to a fever pitch. Additionally, the Union's blockade of the South caused a cotton shortage for English manufacturing. As a result, England, already culturally and economically aligned with the South, tended toward sympathy for the Confederacy at a time of strained diplomatic relations with the Union. Nor did it help Lincoln's cause internationally that his rail-splitter image failed to speak to the British press in the same way that it did the Northern masses. English humor periodicals like *Punch* were consistently and rabidly anti-Lincoln. Instead of recognizing the appeal of a self-made man, British illustrators and satirists considered Lincoln to be "boorish."[29] Indeed, if Lincoln was the representative self-made man, he inhabited all the worst character traits of which British satirists had long mocked in Americans.

Colloquial American speech, for instance, was a perennial target. *Punch* parodied American English by reproducing its seemingly odd pronunciations via phonetic spellings reminiscent of southwestern humor.[30] Plain-talking Lincoln, then, became the leading exemplar of *Punch's* critique of the American butchering of the English language. Consider, for instance, this parody of Lincoln's second inaugural address: "[W]e've done it, gentlemen. Bully for us. Cowhided the Copperheads considerable. *Non nobis*, of course, but still I reckon we have had a hand in the glory, some. . . . Rebellion is a wicked thing, gentlemen, an awful wicked thing, and the mere nomenclating thereof would make my hair stand on end, if it could be more standonender than it is. . . . All very tall talking, gentlemen, but talking won't take Richmond. If it would, and there had been six Richmonds in the field, we should long since have took them all."[31] In addition to mocking Lincoln's looks by referring to his unkempt hair, this imitation pillories the colloquialism ("Bully," "Cowhided"), improper grammar, and neologisms ("standonender") of the American chief executive as representative of uncultured American-ness, in general.

Another London illustrated humor periodical, *Comic News*, imagined the president as an inveterate tobacco chewer, connecting the habit with the demise of the nation-state: "Ah, sir, chewing's one of the great insti-chew-tions of our country, some of our greatest men has chewed in their time. But the old dominion's almost chawed up! The President here emitted from his

"Abraham Africanus the First"

mouth an expectoration of the most alarming magni-chew'd, and shot it with a true and steady aim right on the left boot of your amiable and boot-iful correspondent." Another article chided Lincoln in sing-songy rhyme: "So poor America is ruled, and scolded, and schooled, by a buffoon, a monkey, a wretched old donkey, who is more fit for a flunkey than to rule this great country."[32] Both of these pieces imagine Lincoln as a vulgar "buffoon" who was a representative man of the worst qualities of his countrymen. In *Comic News*, anyway, if he was a model American, he was, to paraphrase Trollope, a bad model. As these examples show, Lincoln's folksy humility and humor did not appeal to Britons (nor to a Southern culture that valued all things English) in the same way that it did to many Northerners in the United States.

Cartoon caricatures in English humor periodicals painted a similar picture of Lincoln as an uncultured rube. For example, John Tenniel's May 9, 1863, *Punch* cartoon "The Great 'Cannon Game'" comments on a Confederate victory over Union naval forces at Charleston (fig. 4.9). It depicts a Neanderthal and racialized Lincoln, with pronounced jaws and

Figure 4.9. "The Great 'Cannon Game.'" *John Tenniel*, Punch *(London), May 9, 1863, 191. HarpWeek.*

vacant eyes, losing at billiards to a dashing Jefferson Davis. In the caption, Lincoln says in an aside, "Darn'd if he ain't scored ag'in!—wish I could make a few *winning* hazards for a change."[33] Tenniel attributed colloquial speech to Lincoln not to identify him as a man of the people but, rather, to portray him as unsophisticated and inept.

Northerners were aware of the discrepancy between Northern and British readings and renderings of Lincoln's image. The 1864 joke book *Old Abe's Jokes, Fresh from Abraham's Bosom* calls attention to this disparity in juxtaposing "An Englishman's Portraits of Old Abe" with "An American's Portrait of Father Abraham" on facing pages. On the left side, the "Englishman's Portraits," quoting from an unnamed source, begins, "To say that he is ugly, is nothing; to add that his figure is grotesque, is to convey no adequate impression." The English "portrait" goes on to describe "long bony arms and legs" that "somehow seem to be always in the way," "a head cocoa-nut shaped and somewhat too small for such a stature, covered with rough, uncombed and uncomable [*sic*] hair, that stands out in every direction at once; a face furrowed, wrinkled and indented, as though it had been scarred by vitrol [*sic*]," accented by "a nose and ears which have been taken by mistake from a head of twice the size." This English version of Lincoln wears "a long, tight, badly-fitting suit of black, creased, soiled and puckered up at every salient point of the figure" with "ill-fitting boots, gloves too long for the long bony fingers, and a fluffy hat, covered to the top with dusty, puffy crape." The "American's Portrait" on the right begins by admitting Lincoln's "awkward speech and yet more awkward silence, his uncouth manners, self-taught and partly forgotten," but it also sees Lincoln "[i]n character and culture" as "a fair representative of the average American," "the type of 'Brother Jonathan [a nineteenth-century predecessor to Uncle Sam],' a not perfect man and yet more precious than fine gold."[34] The descriptions are somewhat similar, but the connotations diverge widely; the American view emphasizes Lincoln as representative of the American people, thus ennobling his imperfections and awkwardness in a way that the English view could not countenance.

James Russell Lowell, in his essay "Abraham Lincoln," similarly accounts for the difference between American and British conceptions of Lincoln: "That Mr. Lincoln is not handsome nor elegant, we learn from certain English tourists. . . . Mr. Lincoln has also been reproached with Americanism by some not unfriendly British critics; but, with all deference, we cannot say that we like him any the worse for it, or see in it any reason why he

"Abraham Africanus the First"

should govern Americans the less wisely." Lowell continues, somewhat defensively, "People of more sensitive organizations may be shocked, but we are glad that in this our true war of independence, which is to free us forever from the Old World, we have had at the head of our affairs a man whom America made, as God made Adam, out of the very earth, unancestried, unprivileged, unknown, to show us how much truth, how much magnanimity, and how much state-craft await the call of opportunity in simple manhood when it believes in the justice of God and the worth of man."[35] Lowell's formulation mirrors that of the joke book: unlike the British, who he implied were unable to understand the importance of Lincoln's storied rise from the people, Lowell saw Lincoln's lack of elegance and his rough-hewn "Americanism" as positive traits for democratic governance.

Lowell's touchiness about British views of Lincoln does call attention to his persistently negative image there. Gary L. Bunker, a scholar of Lincoln's image in political cartoons, claims that "England's image makers were the primary sculptors of his pejorative international reputation."[36] Some British cartoon depictions of Lincoln go further than painting him as a backwoods boor and, mirroring Southern and Copperhead images of Lincoln, associate him directly with evil. Matt Morgan, who drew first for London *Fun* and then for *Comic News*, pictures Lincoln in turns as Satan, Death, and a vampire. First, "Pull Devil—Pull Baker," from the October 8, 1864, *Comic News*, repurposes an old saying (whose origins are unknown) about an intractable argument to describe the 1864 presidential contest, captured in an image of Democratic candidate General George B. McClellan and Lincoln—whose head sprouts horns—tugging on a map of the "Northern States" (fig. 4.10). Depicting Lincoln as the Devil and McClellan as Baker clearly put Morgan (and *Comic News*) in McClellan's camp.[37]

Morgan's "The Vampire," in the November 26, 1864, *Comic News* (fig. 4.11), depicts Lincoln as a vampire hovering over a crouching Columbia, whom he threatens, "Columbia, thou art mine; with thy blood I will renew my lease of life—ah! ah!" (The vampire association is prescient, given the 2012 film *Abraham Lincoln: Vampire Hunter*, which figures the entire Confederacy and its slaveholding dominion as a conspiracy of vampires that Lincoln is trained to defeat.) The drawing propagates the image of Lincoln as a blood-thirsty, inhuman monster, much like the Lincoln-as-Satan images produced in the South. Morgan's "In for His Second Innings," from the December 6, 1864, *Comic News* uses a cricket metaphor to describe the onset of Lincoln's second term and similarly associates Lincoln with the

PULL DEVIL—PULL BAKER.

Figure 4.10. "Pull Devil—Pull Baker." *Matt Morgan*, Comic News, *October 8, 1864, 159.*
Courtesy, The Western Reserve Historical Society, Cleveland, Ohio.

supernaturally undead (fig. 4.12). Lincoln removes his face/mask to reveal
his true self, Death. The masked-evil trope recalls the *Southern Illustrated
News* cartoon "Masks and Faces" in its intimation that Lincoln's visage is a
sham that hides evil intentions (see fig. 4.2). In "In for His Second Innings,"
the body of a fallen soldier lies beneath a broken cannon in the background
to highlight just whom and how Lincoln will reap.[38] Morgan's portraits
of Lincoln are all similarly ghastly in their imagination of him as an evil
antihero full of malice.

Though the British press presented a consistently negative picture of
Lincoln, these images did not reach Southern readers in great numbers.
Because of the Union blockade of the Southern coast, importation of
prints and journals was impractical when not impossible; as such, British
anti-Lincoln caricature minimally impacted Southern residents. But just
how influential were such images to a Northern American audience? *Comic
News*, for one, ran for a mere nineteen months (July 1863 to March 1865)
and has only been recently rediscovered by scholars. *Punch* and *Fun* were
more popular, but it is unclear how widely they circulated in the Northern
states during the war. The realities of transatlantic transportation meant
that the news that *Punch* and other British humor periodicals satirized was

"Abraham Africanus the First"

already weeks old and would be even older by the time American readers saw the satires. Even so, *Punch* did have influence and importance as an "index to current attitudes, prejudices, enthusiasms, phobias." If *Punch* and other British periodicals sought to reflect British public opinion rather than changing it, that reflection was seen across the ocean.[39] If *Punch* and other British periodicals sought to reflect British public opinion rather than changing it, that reflection was seen across the ocean. U.S. General Irvin McDowell expressed a broader anxiety about Britain's estimation of the United States when he told a *New York Times* correspondent that "there was no nation in the world whose censure or praise the people of the United

THE VAMPIRE.

Abe.—"COLUMBIA, THOU ART MINE; WITH THY BLOOD I WILL RENEW MY LEASE OF LIFE—AH! AH!"

Figure 4.11. "The Vampire." *Matt Morgan,* Comic News, *November 26, 1864, 221. Courtesy, The Western Reserve Historical Society, Cleveland Ohio.*

"Abraham Africanus the First"

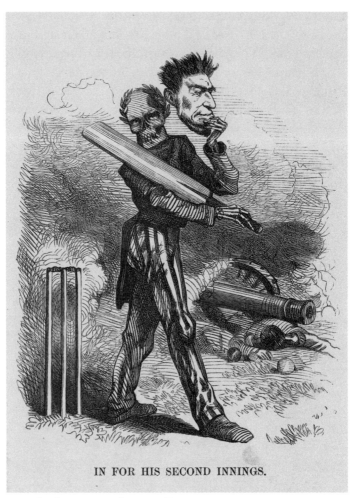

IN FOR HIS SECOND INNINGS.

Figure 4.12. "In for His Second Innings." *Matt Morgan, Comic News, December 6, 1864, 240. Courtesy, The Western Reserve Historical Society, Cleveland, Ohio.*

States care about except England."[40] *Punch* and other British periodicals engaged much more gleefully in censure than in praise of Lincoln as a symbol of the Union.

Even influential British illustrators came to regret their cruel pictorial treatments of Lincoln after his assassination in 1865. In his 1874 collection of cartoons, *The American War*, Morgan omitted some of his more damning images and mollified others with his accompanying text. He also included a nonsatiric cartoon about Lincoln's assassination (originally published in *Fun*), with the commentary, "For once the artist pictures unbiased truth.

"Abraham Africanus the First"

. . . The veil was torn from all eyes, and the Star of Empire shone in the West with an unflecked radiance which has never since worn a cloud."[41] In hindsight, Morgan, in leaving out the cruelest depictions of Lincoln and confessing to previously obfuscating "the unbiased truth," seems to recant his treatment of Lincoln.

Similarly, soon after Lincoln was assassinated, Tenniel published the cartoon "Britannia Sympathises with Columbia" in London *Punch*. In this image, Britannia lays a wreath on Lincoln's deathbed, while Columbia bows her head toward Lincoln's, and an emancipated man, undone shackles next to him, sits on the floor, his head on his knees in grief. The nonsatiric image was accompanied by a long poem, "Abraham Lincoln. Foully Assassinated, April 14, 1865." The poem confesses to misreading Lincoln's workmanlike manner. It begins, self-accusingly.

> *You* lay a wreath on murdered LINCOLN's bier,
> *You*, who with mocking pencil wont to trace,
> Broad for the self-complacent British sneer,
> His length of shambling limb, his furrowed face,
> His gaunt, gnarled hands, his unkempt, bristling hair,
> His garb uncouth, his bearing ill at ease,
> His lack of all we prize as debonair.

This ugliness and "lack of all we prize as debonair," the poet and cartoonist have since learned, expresses not incompetence but strength of will. Lincoln—"This rail-splitter a true-born king of men"—eventually managed to "shame me from my sneer, / To lame my pencil, and confute my pen." The poet, thus, admits his or her mistake and has come to equate Lincoln's simplicity with kingliness. Additionally, the poet, in confessing a transformation from sneering mockery to self-effacing modesty, was apparently trying to become more like Lincoln. The poem proceeds to describe how "[t]hose gaunt, long-laboring limbs were laid to rest!" This line is important, showing as it does the transformation of Lincoln's image in the minds of Tenniel and others: the length of Lincoln's limbs now describes not provincial clumsiness but the physical labor ("long-laboring") of restoring the union.[42]

When the American humor periodical *Frank Leslie's Budget of Fun* reprinted this poem in July 1865, the editors announced that they forgave the "PENITENT PUNCH": "We admit the penitent jester, and in consideration of his confession give him plenary absolution."[43] *Frank Leslie's* felt no need to offer its own apology, despite the fact that it had included countless caricatures of Lincoln—favorable, unfavorable, and merely fun—over the previous five years. This is because caricatures of Lincoln in the American North seem to have worked differently than did *Punch* cartoons. That is, the visual association of a leading figure, such as the president, with humility, labor, physical prowess, and humor was much less unseemly to American cartoonists and readers than to their British counterparts, who finally came to see the positive content of the symbolism of "long-laboring" limbs after four-plus years.

CHAPTER 5

"A Hoosier Michael Angelo": The Politics of Lincoln's Physical Appearance in Popular Media

He has a face like a hoosier Michael Angelo, so awful ugly
it becomes beautiful, with its strange mouth, its deep cut,
criss-cross lines, and its doughnut complexion

—*Walt Whitman*

In one version of a widely circulated story, Lincoln recalled,

In the days when I used to be "on the circuit," I was once accosted in the cars by a stranger, who said, "Excuse me, sir, but I have an article in my possession which belongs to you." "How is that?" I asked, considerably astonished. The stranger took a jack-knife from his pocket. "This knife," said he "was placed in my hands some years ago, with the injunction that I was to keep it until I found a man *uglier* than myself. I have carried it from that time to this. Allow me *now* to say, sir, that I think *you* are fairly entitled to the property."

Though this anecdote, like most Lincoln stories, may well be apocryphal, P. M. Zall, who has collected and analyzed hundreds of such stories, surmises that Lincoln likely did tell this story or something similar. According to painter Francis Carpenter, who retold this story, Lincoln was "always ready to join in a laugh at the expense of his person, concerning which he was very indifferent."[1] Lincoln was not just "indifferent" to conceptions of his physical appearance; indeed, he made political capital of his homeliness by caricaturing himself. Similar self-mockery is at work in a joke attributed to Lincoln in 1858, in which he claimed that he swore he would shoot any man he could find who was uglier than he. When he came across such a man, explained his "sacred oath," and told him he'd better make peace with his maker, the joke goes, the man replied to Lincoln, "Well sir: you are evidently a gentleman & not as I at first supposed some escaped lunatic & sir, you look as if you might put your threat into execution; but sir, all that I have got to say is, If I am any worse looking than you are, for *God's sake shoot me* and git me out of the way!"[2]

Many scholars who study Lincoln in caricature dismiss the bulk of it as particularly cruel to Lincoln, and almost none goes far enough in examining the positive possibilities of image amelioration resulting from Lincoln's own visual and verbal uses of self-satire.[3] As a closer look at popular circulating images of Lincoln shows, his consistent denigrations of his own appearance through modest self-presentation helped to shape satiric representations of him. By preemptively accentuating his physical irregularities, Lincoln to a certain extent guided satirists' depictions, thus mitigating the damage they could do.

Lincoln was unusually tall at six feet four and had limbs out of proportion with the rest of his body; long, bony fingers; huge feet; long ears; a sunken chest; and a gaunt, elongated face. One biographer describes him, "It was less his height that merited special comment . . . than the extraordinary proportions of his long legs, large feet, and, most remarkable of all, his arms. When he stood straight, with his arms at his sides, and his shoulders in their customary droop, the tips of his fingers reached nearly three inches lower than on the normal adult frame."[4] In short, Lincoln's exaggerated physical features meant that his actual appearance was already in a sense a caricature.

The 1864 burlesque campaign biography *The Only Authentic Life of Abraham Lincoln, Alias "Old Abe"* attempts to play on these irregularities. The pamphlet begins its narration of Lincoln's life by announcing that he "was six feet two inches in height" at birth and that "Mr. Lincoln stands six feet twelve in his socks, which he changes once every ten days. His anatomy is composed mostly of bones, and when walking he resembles the offspring of a happy marriage between a derrick and a windmill. . . . His head is shaped something like a ruta-bago, and his complexion is that of a Saratoga trunk. . . . The glove-makers have not yet had time to construct gloves that will fit him." The description is accompanied

"A Hoosier Michael Angelo"

by the picture "Lincoln Out Walking," which though whimsical in its exaggeration of Lincoln's prodigious height—with trees at his waist and clouds at his shoulder to provide scale—is not particularly pejorative (fig. 5.1).[5] The verbal description, of course, cruelly mocks the then-president's physical appearance.

This had been a common tactic during the 1860 campaign as well, as is evidenced by the lyrics of two campaign songs in *The Democratic Campaign Songster*. For example, "O! Poor Abraham!" features the chorus, "O! poor Abraham! your chances are too small, / You'll never be a President—you're too homely, and too tall." The song assumes, incorrectly, that Lincoln's "homely" physical appearance would turn off voters and

Figure 5.1. "Lincoln Out Walking." The Only Authentic Life of Abraham Lincoln, Alias "Old Abe," a Son of the West *(New York: Offices of Comic Monthly, 1864): 14. Courtesy, Lilly Library, Indiana University, Bloomington, Indiana.*

that his looks made him somehow unfit for office. Another song, "Lincoln's Picture," features six verses cataloguing positive images of Lincoln then in circulation, introduced by the refrain "Tell us." The song calls attention to the broader distribution of images of candidates, from photographs to drawings to caricatures, than had been seen in any previous campaign. (*The Democratic Campaign Songster*, for instance, features an illustration of Democratic nominee Stephen A. Douglas on its cover.) For the first time, voters who had never seen the candidates in person could look at a proliferation of their caricatured images in addition to the extant traditions of illustrated campaign newspapers and separately published prints.

The sixth verse of "Lincoln's Picture" proceeds,

> Tell us he resembles Jackson,
> Save he wears a larger boot,
> And is broader 'cross the shoulders,
> And is taller by a foot.

Lincoln's height here is not pilloried, and the rest of the song highlights public perceptions of Lincoln's laboring past, "Seven cords or more per day"; his temperance, "Never drank a glass of whisky"; and his piety, "How each night he seeks his closet, / There, alone, to kneel and pray." But all these ostensible compliments serve merely to set up the last verse, which operates as a sort of punch line to the song.

> Any lie you tell we'll swallow,—
> Swallow any kind of mixture,
> But, O! don't, we beg and pray you,—
> Don't, for God's sake, show his picture.[6]

After identifying previous praise of Lincoln as a "lie" or "mixture," the song feigns fear at being shown Lincoln's likeness because of the singer's horror at Lincoln's homeliness. In the logic of the song, then, exaggerations of the Republican candidate's personal virtues and "lie(s)" about his political acumen and policy are easier to "swallow" than his haggard visage. But, in caricature anyway, Lincoln's picture becomes less hideous as it visually identifies him with working people and against more refined, or dandified, politicians. This could be what Walt Whitman meant when he described Lincoln's face as "so awful ugly it becomes beautiful."[7] Ironically, the ditty's mock fear, thus, may have been more appropriate than its author had imagined.

"A Hoosier Michael Angelo"

Lincoln and his inner circle were as aware of the emerging power of portraiture as they were that he was not an attractive man. His campaign certainly was invested in the emergent power of images. Mary Todd Lincoln allegedly worried about a poor, pre-1860 convention image of Lincoln juxtaposed alongside the portraits of other candidates in a New York illustrated paper, complaining that the picture "couldn't have been made more dismal. Half seriously I said to him: 'A look at that face is enough to put an end to hope.'" Her concerns demonstrate the popular power of illustrated news in terms of electability. Lincoln's backers flooded the nominating convention in Chicago with "hastily printed woodcuts," and Norman B. Judd, a key member of Lincoln's Illinois team, wrote Lincoln in June asking for a profile picture to send to a Philadelphia medal maker: "Every little [bit] helps, and I am coming to believe, that likenesses broad cast, are excellent means of electioneering."[8] Lincoln himself is said to have thanked famous photographer Mathew Brady for the portrait he took during his February 1860 visit to New York for the Cooper Union speech, saying later, "Brady and the Cooper Institute made me President."[9] This image proliferated throughout the campaign season and, along with caricatures, was the chief way in which voters came to visualize Lincoln.

But not all circulating images of Lincoln were as careful or kind. Telegraph operator Albert B. Chandler told *Harper's* that Lincoln told him the following story:

> [S]oon after I was nominated for President at Chicago, I went up one day, and one of the first really distinguished men who waited on me was a picture-man, who politely asked me to favor him with a sitting for my picture. Now at that time there were less photographs of my phiz than at present, and I went straightway with the artist, who detained me but a moment, and took one of the most really life-like pictures I have ever seen of myself. . . . But this stiff, ungovernable hair of mine was all sticking every way, very much as it is now, I suppose; and so the operation of his camera was but "holding the mirror up to nature." I departed, and did not think of pictures again until that evening I was gratified and flattered at the cry of newsboys who had gone to vending the pictures: "Ere's yer last picter of Old Abe! He'll look better when he gets his *hair* combed!"[10]

Lincoln's retelling of a joke that mildly denigrates his unkempt hair—recalling his response to an 1857 bust portrait, which he said "presented me in all [my hair's] fright"—reveals his cognizance of the proliferation of images during the presidential campaign and of the fact that negative images would serve as humorous fodder for his detractors. Lincoln sat for at least eight portrait artists during the 1860 campaign.[11]

Lincoln found a way to parlay his bad looks into political capital through self-effacing mockery. For example, a two-page biography he wrote and sent to friend and political booster J. W. Fell in 1860 ended with a self-mocking physical description: "If any personal description of me is thought desirable, it may be said, I am, in height, six feet, four inches, nearly; lean in flesh, weighing, on an average, one hundred and eighty pounds; dark complexion, with coarse black hair, and grey eyes—no other marks or brands recollected."[12] In a personal sketch intended, undoubtedly, for political use, Lincoln closed with a joke in which he described himself as a farmer would cattle. Lincoln's self-description—with his "dark complexion," "coarse black hair," and his reference to brands—also ironically echoes the rhetoric of want ads for fugitive slaves. In this sense, Lincoln had already sufficiently trod the territory embarked upon by campaign materials burlesquing his appearance and in doing so to a certain extent minimized their bite.

In addition to Lincoln's verbal mockery of his own appearance, he also often appeared unkempt in public—with ill-fitting clothes and hair askew. His pants were "invariably too short, sometimes verging on the ludicrous." He always wore a faded brown hat, and during his debates with Douglas, he eschewed vest and waistcoat. Lincoln's friend Russell H. Conwell recalled seeing Lincoln at the Cooper Union speech and described his "ill-fitting new suit . . . his old hat . . . his protruding wrists . . . the disheveled hair . . . his long legs, his bony face . . . the one-sided necktie." Even after being elected president, he wore a dirty duster on his ambles around the streets of Washington.[13] So, again, when the author of *The Only Authentic Life* claimed tongue-in-cheek of Lincoln, "In his habits he is by no means foppish, though he brushes his hair sometimes, and is said to wash," the joke's ironic rendering of a low standard of personal hygiene and appearance by which to judge Lincoln merely rehashed Lincoln's own personal self-presentation.[14]

Because Lincoln was an ambitious, self-aware politician long before garnering the 1860 Republican nomination, he must have given at least some thought to his image. It could be that politicians were simply not as "image-conscious" as modern politicians.[15] But such an explanation does not account for the fact that so many contemporary observers—both friends and enemies—felt it necessary to comment on Lincoln's pronounced

"A Hoosier Michael Angelo"

uncouthness and disheveled appearance in public, or for the fact that as the Chicago newsboy joke shows, Lincoln was aware both of his public appearance and of others' perceptions of it. Lincoln, thus, may have been more image-conscious than some historians imagine, as he seems to have played up his naturally awkward appearance. For example, when Lincoln wore his famous tall top hat—which in the mid-nineteenth century was a casual instead of a formal gesture—it further elongated his six-feet-four frame. Additionally, when he sought to make a point during a speech, he would reportedly "crouch down [on the lecture platform] and then jump off the ground for emphasis." In the early age of visual media, when political caricature predominated over photographs, he may have acted this way as a "gimmick" or a public relations stunt. Noah Brooks recalled these odd public-speaking mannerisms similarly: "As he reasoned with his audience, he bent his bony form over the railing of the platform, stooping lower and lower as he pursued his argument, until, having reached his point, he clinched it . . . and then suddenly sprang upright, reminding one of the springing open of a jack-knife blade."[16] An 1860 description of Lincoln's oratorical decorum certainly implied intentionality in such antics, suggesting that his experience had taught him well the art of altering his stage persona to achieve different effects: "His manner before a popular assembly is as he pleases to make it, being either superlatively ludicrous, or very impressive. He employs but little gesticulation, but when he desires to make a point, produces a shrug of his shoulders, an elevation of his eyebrows, a depression of his mouth, and a general malformation of countenance so comically awkward that it never fails to 'bring down the house.'"[17] According to this and other accounts, Lincoln scored personality as well as political points by making fun of himself. His strategic employment of "comically awkward" stances was consistent with Lincoln's persistent use of self-satire for political ends.

The political capital Lincoln manufactured out of his gangly stature came, at least in part, through the medium of political cartoons. A contemporary of Lincoln claimed, "The peculiar characteristics of Mr. Lincoln made him a splendid subject. . . . His long arms and legs, his leanness of flesh, his big nose and mouth, and his disheveled hair were distinguishing features for the exaggerations of the cartoonists," who "labored to make him appear ridiculous." Harold Holzer offers Lincoln's homeliness as itself a reason for the plethora of caricatures of him: "We should acknowledge, just as Lincoln often did, that he possessed a face and a frame that seemed crafted for caricature; it hardly required exaggeration. . . . The homely, unusually tall Lincoln looked rather funny just as he was. How could the cartoonists have resisted such a figure? . . . Some cartoons may have attempted to make Lincoln look ridiculous, but he entered the national stage looking rather ridiculous to begin with."[18] If Lincoln "looked rather funny just as he was," there was not much that caricaturists could do to further exaggerate those features. The word "caricature" is derived from the Latin root *carricare*, which means "loaded statement" or "exaggerate." This is what caricature does: it distorts the normal proportions of the body, exaggerates facial expressions to telegraph emotion, and employs visual symbols as ideographical shorthand.[19] This is not, of course, to imply that Lincoln somehow willed himself to be extremely tall, thin, and homely. Rather, since his physical appearance—both his natural attributes and his tousled self-presentation—was in a sense already an exaggeration, in artists' caricatures he may have actually looked less ridiculous because less physically altered by artists than the other subjects caricatured alongside him.

Though there is little hard evidence detailing Lincoln's reactions to or attitudes about political cartoons, we can engage in educated speculation about Lincoln's cognizance of and relationship to caricature.[20] To wit, Lincoln seemed to understand the satiric techniques of political cartoons, as he himself had used such methods, most notably in his 1852 speech mocking Franklin Pierce by drawing a cartoon with words. He began by recalling humorous, self-satirizing anecdotes of Illinois militia parades, including one with "our old friend Gordon Abrams, with a pine wood sword, about nine feet long, and a paste-board cocked hat, from front to rear about the length of an ox yoke, and very much the shape of one turned bottom upwards; and with spurs having rowels as large as the bottom of a teacup, and shanks a foot and a half long. . . . Among the rules and regulations, no man is to wear more than five pounds of cod-fish for epaulets, or more than thirty yards of bologna sausages for a sash." Lincoln then applied a similar burlesque to Pierce that Lincoln could not help but introduce with mocking mimicry of Stephen A. Douglas.

> Now, in the language of Judge Douglas, "I submit to you gentlemen,"
> whether there is not great cause to fear that on some occasion when
> Gen. Scott suspects no danger, suddenly Gen. Pierce will be discovered
> charging upon him, holding a huge roll of candy in one hand for a
> spy-glass; with BUT labelled on some appropriate part of his person;
> with Abrams' long pine sword cutting in the air at imaginary cannon

balls, and calling out "boys there's a game of ball for you," and over all streaming the flag, with the motto, "We'll fight till we faint, and I'll treat when it's over."[21]

Lincoln here narrated the drawing of a political cartoon, complete with captions. While this does not tell us what Lincoln thought of his own image in caricature, it does imply that his impressive satiric repertoire also included the art of visual caricature, even if he did not draw.

Cartoon Race: The 1860 Presidential Campaign

The ameliorative effect of Lincoln's self-constructed homespun image operated even in caricatures intended to represent him pejoratively, especially in the initial "rail-splitter" images of the 1860 campaign. Frank Bellew's "A 'Rail' Old Western Gentleman," for example, which mocks the reliance of Lincoln's campaign on the "rail-splitter" theme, was presumably intended negatively but may not necessarily have appeared as such to its audience. In drawing Lincoln's arms, legs, and torso as banded-together sticks, Bellew implies that Lincoln's candidacy consisted of nothing but those rails. In a sense it echoes a Democratic newspaper in Illinois that claimed tongue-in-cheek that splitting rails seemed to be Lincoln's only qualification for president, "aside from his personal beauty."[22] In disparaging this homespun image, Democrats and Lincoln's other opponents risked offending Americans with humble backgrounds and who identified with Lincoln's laboring past. By capturing Lincoln's unattractive visage and his mussed hair and imagining his spindly body as made of rails, Bellew may have helped to embellish Lincoln's image as a Western Cincinnatus even as he attempted to puncture it.

Lincoln benefited more from cartoons that compared caricatured images of the leading candidates, especially given the striking discrepancy in physical appearance between Lincoln and Democratic challenger Douglas, who was shorter and presented himself as an immaculate gentleman. A Douglas biographer offers the following account of their respective appearances at an 1858 debate in Ottawa, Illinois.

> They presented a striking contrast. Lincoln, tall, angular, and long of limb; Douglas, short, almost dwarfed by comparison, broad-shouldered and thick chested. Lincoln was clad in a frock coat of rusty black, which was evidently not made for his lank, ungainly body. His sleeves did not reach his wrists by several inches, and his trousers failed to conceal his huge feet. . . . Altogether, his appearance bordered

upon the grotesque. . . . Douglas, on the contrary, presented a well-groomed figure. He wore a well-fitting suit of broadcloth; his linen was immaculate; and altogether he had the appearance of a man of the world whom fortune had favored.

Lincoln was by this time a relatively wealthy man and as such could certainly have afforded better-tailored suits and a haircut for a key debate, but he may have recognized the satiric-as-political effects of emphasizing the juxtaposition of the already obvious physical and stylistic differences between himself and Douglas in order to portray himself as a "man of popular origin."[23]

This is apparent in the comparative language Lincoln employed in a July 17, 1858, speech in Springfield. Lincoln began his speech, "Senator Douglas is of world wide renown. All the anxious politicians of his party, or who have been of his party for years past, have been looking upon him as certainly, at no distant day, to be the President of the United States. They have seen in his round, jolly, fruitful face, postoffices, landoffices, marshalships, and cabinet appointments, chargeships and foreign missions, bursting and sprouting out in wonderful exuberance ready to be laid hold of by their greedy hands. [*Great laughter.*]" In this cartoon-like caricature of Douglas's visage, Lincoln connected fame to corruption and nepotism: "On the contrary nobody has ever expected me to be President. In my poor, lean, lank, face, nobody has ever seen that any cabbages were sprouting out."[24] By describing his own face as "poor" and Douglas's as "fruitful," Lincoln characterized physical difference as class distinction, associating himself with the people and Douglas with elites and the sycophants who preyed upon those elites.

Lincoln modestly invoked in 1858 a distinction between his own "poor, lean, lank face" and Douglas's "round" face that would become central to caricaturists' shorthand for the candidates in the 1860 presidential election. "Honest Old Abe and the Little Boy in Search of His Mother—A Sensation Story," from a July 1860 issue of *Phunny Phellow*, a pro-Union humor magazine with low-quality paper and poor typography and layout but excellent political cartoons, effectively captures this difference. Again, because Lincoln's actual physical appearance seemed itself a caricature, it, in some ways, minimized the work that a caricaturist could do in burlesquing it. In the cartoon, Lincoln is depicted as ugly, with wild hair and overly sharp features, but while he carries the identifying ax to split rails, he is, otherwise, not cruelly caricatured, at least when compared to the outlandish image of the man-child Douglas, who is savagely portrayed as

"A Hoosier Michael Angelo"

a pouting child with a "Kansas" feather in his hat, associating him with his 1854 Kansas-Nebraska Act.[25]

The motif of Douglas as a little boy searching for his mother derives from his unorthodox (at the time) decision to actively campaign after being nominated by the Northern Democratic Party. Douglas claimed that he was traveling east to visit his elderly mother but, instead, spent time electioneering in New England. His familial excuse, as well as his short stature, gave satirists all the material they needed to burlesque his motives. For example, the pamphlet *A "Wide Awake" Poem* (1860) claims in its subtitle that it would document "The Wanderings of the Little Giant 'in Search of His Mother.'" The poem describes,

> this *babe* of the West—
> In his best bib and tucker, nice breeches, and vest,
> . . . in search of his mother.

Upon arriving in New England, the "young giant," a play on Douglas's nickname, "the Little Giant"

> came to the clam-bakes, and stopped at the fountains;
> He blustered, and blabbered, and waddled about,
> His mother scarce knowing her darling was out!

In this way, the poem depicts Douglas simultaneously as a petulant child and a sneaky political operator. Lincoln, of course, compares favorably to the image of Douglas put forth in *A "Wide Awake" Poem*. The poet, Almon H. Benedict, admits of Lincoln, "No beauty, 'tis true, but often the case is, / There's *greatness of soul with the plainest of faces*." Here Benedict attempts to refigure Lincoln's homeliness as evidence of his moral fortitude. In this sense, Lincoln was "not like the rover—so oily and pliant" and, therefore, "more of a statesman, he's more of a giant!" These juxtaposed images lead to a punning co-option of Douglas's moniker as "giant": Lincoln, Benedict's poem argues, deserves it more because of his height, his "sound head, and a MIGHT BACKBONE!" which are abstract political qualifications materialized into physical qualities.[26]

The poster "'Boy' Lost!" broadside, on the other hand, borrows the language of a missing persons or fugitive slave advertisement to mock Douglas's self-importance: "Talks a great deal, and very loud; ALWAYS ABOUT HIMSELF. HAS AN IDEA THAT HE IS A CANDIDATE FOR THE PRESIDENCY" (fig. 5.2). Douglas's physical appearance was also, of course, fair game, and his shortness and girth—"He is about five feet nothing in height, and about the same in diameter the other way. He has a red face, short legs, and a large belly"—became metaphors for his childlike obstinacy and soaring ambition.[27] Lincoln, however, could be mocked for being too tall or too ugly, but height and homeliness could not serve as easy shorthand for immaturity. Lincoln was often called "Old Abe," a sobriquet that implies aged wisdom. Lincoln was first given this nickname at age thirty-eight in Chicago, though his friends often note that the label was odd because he never looked nor acted old for his age. After the 1860 election, Lincoln told a visitor, "All through the campaign my friends have been calling me 'Honest Old Abe,' and I have been elected mainly on that cry."[28]

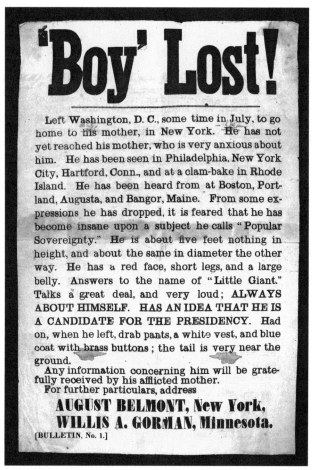

Figure 5.2. "'Boy' Lost!" Undated broadside. *Courtesy, Lilly Library, Indiana University, Bloomington, Indiana.*

"A Hoosier Michael Angelo"

Lincoln's height also gave him an advantage in caricatures that literalized the notion of a political race in their depictions of the candidates. Sporting metaphors for political contests originated in Britain, dating from political cartoons of elections as horse races from the 1760s. As changes in the American electoral system in the early 1800s opened up political participation, politics and sports became linked in the United States as well. Cartoons often featured a candidate in the lead but not yet a winner, thus urging supporters who viewed the image to vote in order to help finish the event. Several 1860 poster cartoons equate Lincoln's lankiness with the ability to win such a sprint. "A Political Race" depicts an enormous Lincoln striding over Douglas's head to take the lead in the race as onlookers cheer (fig. 5.3). Douglas gasps, "I never run so in my life," while John C. Breckinridge, the 1860 Southern Democrat nominee, complains, "That long legged Abolitionist is getting a head of us after all," and a trailing John Bell, the Constitutional Union party nominee, says, "Bless my soul—I give up." None of these candidates comes up even to Lincoln's waist, and, as such, none can hope to keep stride with the "long legged Abolitionist."[29]

Figure 5.3. "A Political Race." Poster cartoon. *New York: Rickey, Mallory, September 1860. Courtesy, Lilly Library, Indiana University, Bloomington, Indiana.*

"Lincoln, Douglas, and the Rail-Fence Handicap," a poster printed in Buffalo, New York, in July 1860, offers a similar image, with Lincoln easily leaping over a huffing and puffing Douglas on the way to the White House (fig. 5.4). In this cartoon, however, there is an obstacle on the race course: a rail fence. Whereas Douglas wonders, "How can I get over this Rail Fence," Lincoln carries a maul and replies, "It can't stop me for I built it." Sport-themed cartoons often "asked voters to cast their ballot for the most manly candidate" at a time when the vote was limited to a white, male polity.[30] Lincoln's laboring past and noted athletic prowess as captured by caricaturists certainly aided viewers in making such decisions.

In both posters. Lincoln is two to three times taller than the other candidates, though his head is approximately the same size as the others'. Caricatures generally tend to increase the proportion of head size to body size, often making it account for one-quarter or more of total body size instead of the more anatomically correct one-eighth.[31] But, in

Figure 5.4. "Lincoln, Douglas, and the Rail-Fence Handicap." Poster cartoon. *Buffalo, NY, July 1860. Library of Congress.*

"A Hoosier Michael Angelo"

emphasizing Lincoln's lankiness, these cartoons keep his head in fairly normal proportion to his body, especially when compared to the squat bodies and huge heads of the other candidates depicted. "May the Best Man Win—Uncle Sam Reviewing the Army of Candidates for the Presidential Chair," discussed below, effectively captures this difference (fig. 5.5). This cartoon compares Lincoln and the other candidates for the 1864 election. The "race" metaphor also continued in 1864, as evidenced by a pro-Lincoln song whose chorus is

> O clear the track for Honest Abe,
> McClellan is behind him,
> He can never win the race,
> He can't keep up with Lincoln.

In "May the Best Man Win," most of the candidates pictured have enormous heads and pudgy bodies. Again, while Lincoln's head is not much larger than those of the others, he is much taller and, therefore, looks more correctly proportioned.[32] In this way, Lincoln escaped a common ploy of caricaturists; his unusual height seemed to save his image from some of the usually negative attributes of caricature.

Figure 5.5. "May the Best Man Win—Uncle Sam Reviewing the Army of Candidates for the Presidential Chair." *Thomas Nast, Phunny Phellow, April 1864, 8–9. Courtesy, The Rare Book and Manuscript Library, University of Illinois at Urbana-Champaign.*

"Long Abe a Little Longer":
The Growth of Lincoln's Image

Cartoon depictions of Lincoln after he became president continued to play up the folksy qualities that had constituted their portrayal of the western "rail-splitter" candidate. Even when Lincoln by virtue of his position became the very type of "great man" that he had attacked Douglas for being in 1858, he was able to maintain his image as a rustic, self-made man. Over the next four years, Lincoln's rail-splitter image would fuse with standard American symbols of authority and patriotism, such that the symbolism of "greatness" itself changed.

Early in 1864, whether Lincoln could win reelection was still very much in doubt; a series of decisive Union victories on the battlefield, though, eventually ensured a landslide over Democratic candidate General George B. McClellan. Caricatures also seem to have aided Lincoln's bid for reelection, often by making Lincoln's prodigious height a metaphor for his sustainability and greatness as a leader.[33] Lincoln was obviously a better-known commodity when he stood for reelection, yet political cartoonists continued to draw, and draw on, his height as a visual metaphor: in 1864 it came to stand more for his growing authority and stature than for his ability to win a political race.

For example, Bellew's "Presidential Cobblers and Wire-Pullers Measuring and Estimating Lincoln's Shoes," in the March 5, 1864, *New York Illustrated News*, an illustrated newspaper in the ilk of *Frank Leslie's Illustrated Newspaper* and *Harper's Weekly*, depicts a hoard of parties, in the act of measuring Lincoln's shoes, interested in challenging his hold on the presidency (fig. 5.6). But, since these "Cobblers and Wire-Pullers"—including the editors of various New York newspapers—are pictured as Lilliputians, they are discovering that Lincoln's are "big shoes to fill."[34] In using the fact that Lincoln had large feet as a way to literalize this cliché, Bellew implies that those who sought to replace Lincoln were not up to the gargantuan responsibilities of the job. As in previous examples, the sleeping Lincoln appears to be of normal proportions while many of the tiny "Cobblers and Wire-Pullers" all have heads that make up over a third of their height.

Lincoln was once again fortunate in 1864 to run against a much-shorter Democratic opponent: General McClellan was known as "Little Mac." Caricaturists were quick to capitalize on the eight-inch height difference between the candidates; as they had with Douglas, cartoonists

"A Hoosier Michael Angelo"

PRESIDENTIAL COBBLERS AND WIRE-PULLERS MEASURING AND ESTIMATING LINCOLN'S SHOES;
INCLUDING BENNETT, HUDSON, GREELEY, RAYMOND, WEED, SEWARD BROOKS, SUMNER, FORNEY, AND MISS ANNA DICKENSON

Figure 5.6. "Presidential Cobblers and Wire-Pullers Measuring and Estimating Lincoln's Shoes." *Frank Bellew, New York Illustrated News, March 5, 1864, 297. Courtesy, American Antiquarian Society.*

evoked McClellan's smallness by picturing him as a child and Lincoln as an adult. For example, Thomas Nast's "May the Best Man Win" compares Lincoln and the other candidates for the 1864 election (see fig. 5.5). Like Douglas before him, the five-feet-eight McClellan is depicted as a boy, here seen glowering over a toy drum. Because of his stature and the toy drum, McClellan's military uniform looks more like a child's dress-up costume than a symbol of respect and prowess. Similarly, in Bellew's "The Good Uncle and the Naughty Boy," from the December 1864 *Frank Leslie's Budget of Fun,* Lincoln and Uncle Sam, towering over a crying McClellan, admonish him for conspiring with the Confederacy, depicted as another boy (fig. 5.7).[35] In both cases, Lincoln's height advantage leads the cartoonist to visualize him as more mature than McClellan, who is drawn as a petulant child.

In September 1864, "This Reminds Me of a Little Joke" appeared in *Harper's Weekly,* which supported Lincoln steadfastly throughout the 1864 campaign (see fig. 1.6). In Bellew's cartoon, a gigantic Lincoln holds the diminutive McClellan in the palm of his hand. Lincoln's comment "This reminds me of a little joke" was often attributed to Lincoln as a nod to his noted (either celebrated or vilified) sense of humor and penchant for telling

Figure 5.7. "The Good Uncle and the Naughty Boy." *Frank Bellew,* Frank Leslie's Budget of Fun, *December 1, 1864, 16. HarpWeek.*

stories. More noteworthy here is the size difference between Lincoln and McClellan.[36] One key difference between images like "This Reminds Me of a Little Joke" and "May the Best Man Win" and those of Lincoln from the 1860 campaign is that Lincoln—though still folksy— is now also associated with the symbols of American government instead of those of a rural outsider. But even as an "establishment" candidate in 1864, Lincoln benefited from caricatured portrayals of him as a fun-loving, rough-hewn westerner; these now-familiar images of Lincoln commingled with markers of officialdom—the suit, the desk—rather than being replaced entirely by those markers.

"A Hoosier Michael Angelo"

After the November elections, several cartoonists depicted Lincoln's size as increasing, a lengthening that corresponds to that of his tenure in office as well as his growing reputation. The most striking example of this visual metaphor is Bellew's "Long Abraham Lincoln a Little Longer," in *Harper's Weekly* on November 26, 1864, soon after the election (fig. 5.8). This image is simultaneously the biggest exaggeration of Lincoln's physical attributes *and* the most respectful, dignified treatment of the president of all the cartoons surveyed in this chapter. Such an apparent contradiction is possible because Bellew exaggerates Lincoln's length in order to pay him respect, associating his height with his endurance as a leader and for his impressive and increasing list of achievements. This cartoon is evidence that if, as one scholar of political cartoons argues, "a cartoon is really an exaggeration to get at an underlying truth," that truth need not always be critical of the exaggerated subject. Indeed, cartoonists may use the same exaggeration to get at different truths.[37] Whereas in the 1860 election Lincoln's height became a visual metaphor for his ability to win a political race, that height, in and after the 1864 campaign, was re-rendered as a metaphor for Lincoln's greatness.

Another postelection cartoon aptly captures how Lincoln could be both praised and maligned in caricature or, rather, praised as imperfect. "With All Thy Faults" is a two-page spread in the *Phunny Phellow* of January 1865 (fig. 5.9). The cartoon depicts Columbia and Lincoln sharing a poignant moment; Columbia holds Lincoln's hand and says, "With all thy faults I love thee still!" Lincoln is huge, folded into his chair, with tousled hair and an appropriately serious countenance. This scene and Columbia's words aptly summarize the Lincoln image in caricature: flawed but earnest and competent, full of integrity. The difference between this 1865 exchange between Lincoln and Columbia and the 1860 exchange in "Good Gracious, Abraham Lincoln" is quite striking and effectively captures the changes that Lincoln's image underwent over four years (see fig. 3.5). In "With All Thy Faults," Columbia, instead of drawing back aghast as she does in "Good Gracious, Abraham Lincoln," leans toward Lincoln, tenderly holds his hand, and looks into his eyes. Lincoln, instead of wryly smiling and carrying rails, sits in a chair in his office—behind him are books and a U.S. map on the wall that says, "THE UNION FOREVER"—and he looks serious, careworn, presidential.[38]

"Jeff Davis's November Nightmare" from the December 3, 1864, *Frank Leslie's Illustrated Newspaper* applies similar visual language but imagines the Confederate perspective on Lincoln's reelection (fig. 5.10). By placing Lincoln on an aged Jefferson Davis's bed (possibly his deathbed) as a manifestation

Figure 5.8. "Long Abraham Lincoln a Little Longer." *Frank Bellew,* Harper's Weekly, *November 26, 1864, 768. Courtesy, American Antiquarian Society.*

Columbia—"With all thy faults I love thee still!"

Figure 5.9. "With All Thy Faults." Phunny Phellow, *January 1865, 8–9. Library Company of Philadelphia.*

of Davis's "nightmare," the cartoon captures the South's disappointment at Lincoln's reelection, which meant that the war would likely continue until the rebellion was crushed. A decrepit Davis asks, "Is that You, still there LONG ABE?" Lincoln, responds, "Yes! And I'm going to be FOUR YEARS LONGER." The text operates through a simple pun on "long," which in reference to Lincoln came to mean both size and duration in office. Lincoln here is again drawn as very "long"—he and his folded-up legs barely fit on Davis—and, as the dialogue informs us, getting longer, apparently so long as to be able to reach into Davis's dreams.[39]

Finally, "The Tallest Ruler on the Globe," in *Frank Leslie's Budget of Fun* in April 1865, just before Lincoln's assassination, also makes Lincoln's height into a metaphor for his greatness as a leader (fig. 5.11). In this very busy cartoon, Lincoln, wearing a wreath to symbolize peace, appears at his inauguration, welcomed by all the symbols of patriotism: Columbia, the American eagle, flags, the Thirteenth Amendment, and the Emancipation Proclamation. Generals Ulysses S. Grant and William T. Sherman and Admiral David Farragut march in the background with trophies representing their conquests. The attendant figures are other world leaders, who are represented as much smaller, dwarfed by Lincoln's greatness. The caption describes the scene: "The tallest ruler on the globe is Inaugurated at Washington—the lesser luminaries of Europe assisting deferentially." These "lesser luminaries" all rave about Lincoln's size. Napoleon III says,

Figure 5.10. "Jeff Davis's November Nightmare." Frank Leslie's Illustrated Newspaper, *December 3, 1864, 176. Courtesy, American Antiquarian Society.*

"Shade of MON UNCLES! How he has GROWN!" while Britannia claims, "Goodness me! Yes! and he keeps on GROWING!" and a sultan invokes Allah and says, "May his shadow never be less."[40] As in other cartoons of 1864 and 1865, Lincoln's size had increased in the nation's and other nations' eyes, becoming a physical manifestation of his excellence. This image shows that even before his assassination, Lincoln had already become a larger-than-life icon, a symbol of the perseverance of the Union.

"A Phenomenon of Portraiture": Complimentary Caricature
The comic press itself joked about the fluidity of Lincoln's image during the 1860 and 1864 presidential campaigns. William Newman's "A

"A Hoosier Michael Angelo"

Phenomenon of Portraiture," published in *Frank Leslie's Budget of Fun* on December 15, 1860, is a kind of metacartoon that reflects on the activity of caricature and its political influence (fig. 5.12). The series of images imagines portraits of Lincoln transforming with his improving political fortunes. The accompanying text explains the transformation. At left, he "looks hideous—cadaverous—repulsive"; at center, "As his chances improve so do his looks. He is now tolerable"; at right, "Being chosen, he grows quite handsome—even angelic."[41] Of course, such an alteration raises a potentially unanswerable chicken-and-egg question. That is, did Lincoln's visage become tolerable and "even angelic" only after his political fortunes improved, or did the changing depictions of Lincoln in some way affect those fortunes? The cartoon speaks to the malleability of the images of public figures in caricature and implies, whether intentionally or not, the power of the comic press in creating and continuously updating those images. It also attests to the ways in which caricature—combined with the momentum of the Republican campaign—may have enhanced Lincoln's image over time instead of debasing it.

Figure 5.11. "The Tallest Ruler on the Globe." *William Newman,* Frank Leslie's Budget of Fun, *April 1865. Courtesy, American Antiquarian Society.*

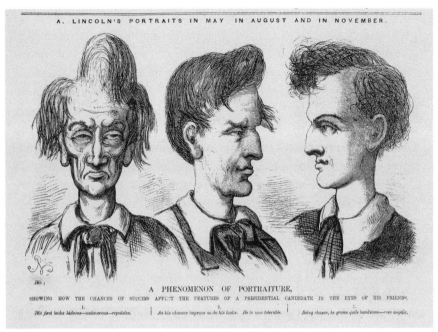

A PHENOMENON OF PORTRAITURE,

SHOWING HOW THE CHANCES OF SUCCESS AFFECT THE FEATURES OF A PRESIDENTIAL CANDIDATE IN THE EYES OF HIS FRIENDS.

1.   2.   3.

His first looks hideous—cadaverous—repulsive. | *As his chances improve so do his looks. He is now tolerable.* | *Being chosen, he grows quite handsome—even angelic.*

Figure 5.12. "A Phenomenon of Portraiture." *William Newman*, Frank Leslie's Budget of Fun, *December 15, 1860, 8. Courtesy, American Antiquarian Society.*

This is antithetical to the way in which caricature is normally assumed to function. Because caricaturists exaggerate and deform their subjects, most critics see caricature as an always-aggressive gesture with an always-punitive result. One scholar considers how caricature's "debunking" may help make public figures seem more approachable and "human"; but, he warns, "This must be weighed against the loss of prestige. The gain of humanness may contribute to the positive image of a figure but detract in other and more crucial political areas."[42] As the above examples reveal, Lincoln was able to avoid this attendant "loss of prestige" when caricatured. This is mainly because Lincoln's reputation, as he shaped it from his earliest days in politics, in no way rested upon the notion of prestige. In his political self-fashioning, Lincoln consistently abdicated prestige in himself and attacked it in others in order to visually and verbally associate himself with the voting masses.

Considering how Lincoln's self-satire and self-presentation may have guided, influenced, or altered the meaning of caricatures challenges the common critical assumption that caricature is an inherently negative gesture. Sometimes, in fact, caricatured pictures of a subject's physical eccentricities can have a positive effect on the subject's image. Lincoln is a perfect example of this. Physical qualities that should be seen as negatives—Lincoln's homely face, his ill-fitting clothes, his rough-hewn self-presentation, and especially his remarkable height—were often rendered in Lincoln caricatures as, at worst, innocuous and, at best, advantageous. Lincoln the satirist-satirized abetted this reversal of the standard iconography of caricature through good-humored self-mockery and a modest demeanor that redefined his humble origins and unusual physical appearance as appropriately "presidential." As A. Ward Jr. put it on the front page of the August 1864 campaign newspaper *Father Abraham*, "A. L. is the cheef among the 43 thousan, and the 1 altogether luvly. As Pres I am bound to admit that he's Gorjeous."[43]

Notes

Bibliography

Index

Notes

Introduction: Abraham Lincoln and
the American Satiric Tradition

1. Bellew, "National Joker," 16.

2. I borrow Stephen Greenblatt's term "self-fashioning" to emphasize the extent to which Lincoln participated in the creation and dissemination of his public image as a "control mechanism" and to highlight the centrality of such self-presentation in popular media to the contemporary and historical perpetuation of Lincoln's image. Greenblatt, *Renaissance Self-Fashioning*, 3.

3. Winter, "Laughing Doves," 1578. See also Blair, *Horse Sense*, and Rourke, *American Humor.*

4. "Yankee Humor," 330.

5. Vinton, "Who Are Our American Humorists?" 1159; Trent, "Retrospect of American Humor," 32–46; J. C. Harris, "Humor in America," 46–49; "English Satire," 1; "Political Satire and Satirists," 621.

6. Hannay, *Satire and Satirists*, ix.

7. J. C. Harris, "Humor in America," 46.

8. Edward Rosenheim Jr. offers a similar view of satire in a 1964 forum in the now-defunct *Satire Newsletter.*

> Of satiric works, it seems to me, we can always say two things: (1) their achievement may be described as an attack (or criticism or exposure or ridicule or spoof), and (2) the attack proceeds by methods which are manifestly not those of direct, literal

communication (and thus involves what has been variously described as obliquity, indirection, irony, invention, distortion, etc., etc.). This seems to me the most basic statement of what the writings that most of us call satire have in common. And I do not think that such writings must necessarily involve a positive exhortation to do or believe what is right or even a direct statement of affirmative principles or norms. ("Norms, Moral and Other," 22)

9. Charles E. Schutz precedes me in labeling Lincoln as a "satyr-statesman," for whom a gentle form of satire is essential to life and politics. The political comedy of Abraham Lincoln is a comedy of politics, and Abraham Lincoln, the humorist, is the supreme politician; each is but the reverse of the other." *Political Humor*, 143. On Franklin as "Homespun," see T. Thompson, "Invectives."

10. Frye, *Anatomy of Criticism*, 226–27; Blair, *Horse Sense*, vi, 5.

11. Elliott, *Power of Satire*, 98; Jameson, *Fables of Aggression*, 138.

12. Dustin Griffin, for example, claims that "satirists' concerns are more *literary* than political" because, in his view, satirists are not committed to a clear set of ideological or political principles. As a result, Griffin ends up following New Critics in asserting that satire cannot "alter the attitudes of its readers" but, instead, more often "reinforces existing attitudes." *Satire*, 150, 154, 155.

13. Burke, *Grammar of Motives*, 514, 512.

14. Burke, "Why Satire," 317.

15. Zall, *Abe Lincoln's Legacy*, xii; Carwardine, *Lincoln*, 49; Tandy, *Crackerbox*, ix.

16. This characterization of American satire corresponds to Mikhail Bakhtin's assertion that Socrates's "dialogic means of seeking truth is counterposed to *official* monologism, which pretends to *possess a ready-made truth*, and it is also counterposed to the naïve self-confidence of those people who think that they know something, that is, who think that they possess certain truths." *Problems*, 110, original emphasis. Bakhtin's work on the dialogic nature of utterances has been attractive to recent theorists of satire. See Griffin, *Satire*; Palmeri, *Satire*; Johnson, *Satire*, 16–17.

17. Schutz, *Political Humor*, 152; Nicolay, *Personal Traits*, 359. Such satiric leveling is akin to Bakhtin's concept of "carnival laughter" in Renaissance Europe, wherein a "temporary suspension, both ideal and real, of hierarchical rank" allowed for free expression and radical social leveling. *Rabelais*, 11, 2, 10. On the concept of the carnival as a descriptor of nineteenth-century political and social relationships, see Reynolds, *Beneath the American Renaissance*, 444.

18. J. C. Harris, "Humor in America," 48–49.
19. See Thomas, *"Lincoln's Humor"*; Bray, "Power to Hurt," 39–58; Zall, *Abe Lincoln Laughing*; Zall, *Abe Lincoln's Legacy*; Zall, *Lincoln on Lincoln*.
20. See Burlingame, *Abraham Lincoln*; Carwardine, *Lincoln*; Kaplan, *Lincoln*; Blegen, *Lincoln's Imagery*; D. L. Wilson, *Lincoln's Sword*; D. L. Wilson, *Lincoln before Washington*; McPherson, "How Lincoln Won," 87–102; Bray, *Reading with Lincoln*.
21. See Harper, *Lincoln and the Press*; Bunker, *From Rail-Splitter to Icon*; Bunker, "Old Abe"; Bunker, "*Comic News*"; Holzer, *Mirror Image*; Holzer, *Lincoln Seen*; Holzer, Boritt, and Neely, *Lincoln Image*; Neely, Holzer, and Boritt, *Confederate Image*.

1. *"This Reminds Me of a Little Joke": From Humor to Satire*

1. Zall, *Abe Lincoln Laughing*, 3.
2. "President and the Office-Seekers," 87; Emerson, "Plain Man," 32; Raymond, *Life and Public Services*, 720; Burt, "Lincoln on His Own Story-Telling," 502; Depew, "Chauncey Depew," 427–28; Nathaniel Grigsby quoted in Wilson and Davis, *Herndon's Informants*, 114–15; D. L. Wilson, *Lincoln's Sword*, 147, original emphasis.
3. Rosenheim, "Norms, Moral and Other," 22.
4. Griffin, *Satire*, 120–32, original emphasis.
5. Bray, *Reading with Lincoln*, 19–23, 87–88; McPherson, "How Lincoln Won," 89; Kaplan, *Lincoln*, 64, 66; Berkelman, "Lincoln's Interest in Shakespeare," 303.
6. Berkelman, "Lincoln's Interest in Shakespeare," 310; Kaplan, *Lincoln*, 66. Bray points out that Lincoln most likely read one of several editions of Aesop's fables printed in Philadelphia by R. Aitken, which began with the first American edition in 1777. These versions also included other sources and extensive morals. Bray, *Reading with Lincoln*, 20.
7. Quoted in Zall, *Abe Lincoln's Legacy*, 28; *Ye Book of Copperheads*, 5.
8. Speed, *Reminiscences*, 31–32; Zall, *Abe Lincoln's Legacy*, 68. Bray counts three recorded uses of Aesop's fables by Lincoln. *Reading with Lincoln*, 21.
9. Lincoln, *Collected Works*, 2:467, original emphasis.
10. Kaplan, *Lincoln*, 273.
11. Burlingame, *Abraham Lincoln*, 1:460.
12. J. H. Cheney, quoted in Stevens, *Reporter's Lincoln*, 53; Hambrecht manuscripts; Bray, "What Abraham Lincoln Read," 58, 71.
13. Zall, *Abe Lincoln's Legacy*, 26–27; Dahlgren, *Memoir*, 370.
14. Zall, *Abe Lincoln's Legacy*, 66; Minier, "Geo. W. Minier," 189–90; Burlingame, *Abraham Lincoln*, 1:431; Ivan Doig, "Genial White House Host," 311. Lincoln owned a copy of the *Letters of Jack Downing* and, according

to Robert B. Rutledge's testimony, "took great pleasure in reading" it. Rutledge to Herndon, Oskaloosa, November 30, 1866, in *Herndon's Informants*, 427.

15. Lincoln, *Collected Works*, 3:279.
16. Burlingame, *Abraham Lincoln*, 1:445.
17. Lincoln, *Collected Works*, 3:298.
18. "Humors of the Day," 339; "Crooked," 355; Zall, *Abe Lincoln's Legacy*, 51.
19. Stewart, "Joseph Glover Baldwin," 230, 379. Bray, on the other hand, sees the case that Lincoln owned and loved Baldwin as somewhat "weaker." *Reading with Lincoln*, 194.
20. Zall, *Abe Lincoln's Legacy*, 91; "Editor's Drawer," 1867, 537–38; Carpenter, "Anecdotes."
21. Herndon and Weik, *Herndon's Lincoln*, 62n; G. W. Harris, *Sut Lovingood*, 48–59; Cook, "Camp Meetings," 61–62; quoted in Zall, *Abe Lincoln's Legacy*, 46.
22. Silver, *Minstrelsy and Murder*, 22; Paxton, *Stray Yankee in Texas*, 113–14, original emphasis. Walter Blair, in particular, has emphasized this connection: "Lawyers, in particular, cherished good stories in which the vernacular figured prominently." *Native American Humor*, 72–73.
23. Justus, introduction, 7.
24. Piacentino, "Intersecting Paths," 15; Justus, introduction, 1–10; Justus, *Fetching the Old Southwest*, 47–73, 66–67; D. L. Wilson, *Lincoln's Sword*, 143.
25. Silver, *Minstrelsy and Murder*, 18; Justus, introduction, 7; Caron, "Backwoods Civility," 163, 182.
26. On Silence Dogood as a persona, see T. Thompson, "Representative Nobodies," 456–63.
27. Burlingame, *Abraham Lincoln*, 1:114; Carwardine, *Lincoln*, 16–18.
28. Lincoln, *Collected Works*, 1:293n4, 295–96.
29. Lincoln, *Collected Works*, 1:297, 295. Lincoln had previously played with Democratic accusations of Whig pretentiousness, for instance, a January 1835 editorial that, according to Lincoln biographer Michael Burlingame, can probably be attributed to Lincoln, claims, "The thing was funny, and we Aristocrats enjoyed it 'hugely.'" *Abraham Lincoln*, 1:96.
30. Lincoln, *Collected Works*, 1:291–92n2, 300n4; D. L. Wilson, *Lincoln's Sword*, 34. Kaplan describes the situation as the "sort of mutually exciting political activity that had provided the context for the start of their courtship during the 1840 presidential campaign." *Lincoln*, 140.
31. Huntzicker, *Popular Press*, 108; D. L. Wilson, *Lincoln's Sword*, 33; Burlingame, *Abraham Lincoln*, 1:95, 96, 107.

32. See Bray, *Reading with Lincoln*, 201; Hambrecht Manuscripts. Kaplan comments that, as president, Lincoln was "rarely without a volume of the mid-nineteenth-century dialect humor he favored for comic relief, whether for nighttime reading or for reciting at lugubrious cabinet meetings." *Lincoln*, 346.

33. Welles, *Diary*, 333. For a synthesis of accounts of Lincoln's use of humor for therapeutic relief from the cares of his responsibilities, see Bray, *Reading with Lincoln*, 201–2.

34. Brooks, "Personal Reminiscences of Lincoln," 564–65; Harper, *Lincoln and the Press*, 187; Rice, *Reminiscences*, 448–49, original emphasis.

35. Conwell, *Why Lincoln Laughed*, 118–19; Carwardine, *Lincoln*, 48.

36. R. B. Browne, *Lincoln-Lore*, xi; Holzer, *Lincoln Seen*, 107.

37. "Great and Astonishing Trick," 16; Bellew, "National Joker," 16; Baker, "Columbia Demands Her Children!"

38. Howard, "I Knew Him."

39. "Hey, Uncle Abe"; *Abraham Africanus*, 30.

40. C. H. Smith, *Bill Arp*, 23, 26.

41. Quoted in Zall, *Abe Lincoln's Legacy*, 27.

42. "Reprinted Letter," 2.

43. "Frank Leslie to the Budgetarians," 1; Conwell, *Why Lincoln Laughed*, 122.

44. *Old Abe's Jokes*, 35, 104. Zall describes *Old Abe's Jokes* as a "cesspool of apocrypha, with clippings from the popular press . . . that defy authentication." *Abe Lincoln's Legacy*, 33.

45. Bellew, "This Reminds Me of a Little Joke," 608.

46. As one scholar of Civil War cartoons puts it, "any symbol, for the detached observer, is in itself without tendency. This observation is borne out by the fact that cartoonists working for opposed factions may employ the same symbols. . . . The symbols become charged when the cartoonist employs them in an appeal to the passions and sentiments of his contemporary culture. Then the reader perceives immediately which symbols the propagandist intends to be positive and which negative, which symbols are to be praised and which damned." Lively, "Propaganda Techniques," 101.

47. Zall, *Abe Lincoln Laughing*, 2. For a synopsis of the approach and politics of Frank Leslie's *Budget of Fun*, see West, "*Budget of Fun*."

48. *Old Abe's Jokes*, 94; Adderup, *Lincolniana*, 54; *Old Abe's Joker*, 21.

49. *New York Post*, February 17, 1864, 1; *New York Herald*, February 19, 1864, 5.

50. *Old Abe's Joker*, preface, n.p.

51. Lentricchia, *Criticism and Social Change*, 79; Lincoln, *Collected Works*, 8:393; Lentricchia, *Criticism and Social Change*, 81.

52. Carwardine, *Lincoln*, 269; Hay, *At Lincoln's Side*, 51; Halpine, *Life and Adventures*, 55, 61. According to Bray, Lincoln may have owned a copy of Halpine's book. "What Abraham Lincoln Read," 53.

53. Hay, *At Lincoln's Side*, 241, original emphasis, 68–69; Zall, *Abe Lincoln's Legacy*, 29.

54. Brooks, "Personal Reminiscences," 567; Lincoln, *Collected Works*, 8:154–55, original emphasis; Harper, *Lincoln and the Press*, 182.

55. Lincoln, *Collected Works*, 8:333. Lincoln had long used this rhetorical formulation to attack slavery. See, for example, *Collected Works*, 1:411–12, 2:405, 3:204–5. For a thorough account of how Lincoln used writing—and meticulous drafting—to shape and test his thinking, see D. L. Wilson, *Lincoln's Sword*.

56. Mitgang, *Abraham Lincoln*, x; Herndon and Weik, *Herndon's Lincoln*, 80; McGill, *American Literature*, 5. See also Burlingame, *Abraham Lincoln*, 2:287–89, 400–401; and Zall, *Abe Lincoln's Legacy*, xiv.

2. "Little Big Man": Modesty and Attack in Lincoln's Writings and Speeches

1. Lincoln, *Collected Works*, 4:62.
2. Ibid., 4:65; Sandage, *Born Losers*, 82.
3. de Certeau, *Practice of Everyday Life*, 37.
4. Ford, *History of Illinois*, 199; Bray, "Power to Hurt," 43.
5. Letter recounting Lincoln's childhood, Blair Manuscripts; Herndon and Weik, *Herndon's Lincoln*, 80.
6. Burlingame, *Abraham Lincoln*, 1:113–14.
7. Lincoln, *Collected Works*, 1:65–66; Bray, "Power to Hurt," 53; Jameson, *Fables*, 138.
8. Northrup Frye derives his conception of irony from Aristotle's *Nichomachean Ethics*, wherein, in Frye's words, "the *eiron* is the man who deprecates himself, as opposed to the *alazon*. Such a man makes himself invulnerable, and . . . there is no question that he is a predestined artist, just as the *alazon* is one of his predestined victims." *Anatomy of Criticism*, 40. On Socratic irony, see Highet, *Anatomy of Satire*, 56–63.
9. Lincoln, *Collected Works*, 1:61–62, 67, original emphasis.
10. Ibid., 1:62.
11. Joshua Speed statement for William Herndon, (by 1882), in Wilson and David, *Herndon's Informants*, 589; Lincoln quoted in Burlingame, *Abraham Lincoln* 1:105; Herndon and Weik, *Herndon's Lincoln*, 116.
12. Herndon and Weik, *Herndon's Lincoln*, 128–29; James H. Matheny, interview by William H. Herndon, 1865–66, in Wilson and Davis, *Herndon's Informants*, 472.

13. Ninian W. Edwards, interview by William H. Herndon, 1865–66, in Wilson and Davis, *Herndon's Informants*, 447.
14. Shackford, *David Crockett*, 52–53.
15. John M. Scott, "Lincoln on the Stump and at the Bar," in Scott to Ida Tarbell, Bloomington, Illinois, August 14, 1895, Tarbell Papers, Allegheny College.
16. For an in-depth treatment of Lincoln's use of invective and billingsgate in political speech in the early part of his career, see Burlingame, *Inner World*, 150–61.
17. Herndon and Weik, *Herndon's Lincoln*, 130.
18. Lincoln, *Collected Works*, 1:509–10. Legend had it that Cass broke his sword rather than surrender it after a battle in the War of 1812. Klunder, *Lewis Cass*, 13.
19. Woodford, *Lewis Cass*, 264; Palmeri, *Satire*, 10, 12; Lincoln, *Collected Works*, 1:514.
20. Crockett, *Autobiography*, 71, 140.
21. *Only Authentic Life*, 4; *Lincoln Catechism*, 37–38.
22. Lincoln, *Collected Works*, 4:64; Winkle, *Young Eagle*, 91.
23. Lincoln, *Collected Works*, 1:508.
24. Ibid., 1:509.
25. Woodford, *Lewis Cass*, 266.
26. Lincoln, *Collected Works*, 1:512–14.
27. Ibid., 1:509.
28. Zall, *Lincoln on Lincoln*, 74–75; Poore, "Benjamin Perley Poore," 221; Burlingame, *Abraham Lincoln*, 1:261.
29. Herndon and Weik, *Herndon's Lincoln*, 384–85; Rugg, *Abraham Lincoln*, 5; Lincoln, *Collected Works*, 2:5–7; Hanna, *Abraham among the Yankees*, 73.
30. Lincoln, *Collected Works*, 2:146, original emphasis, 149, editorial addition in original; Caron, "Backwoods Civility," 172.
31. Zall, *Abe Lincoln's Legacy*, xvii.
32. Lincoln, *Collected Works*, 2:136, 144, 156; Kaplan, *Lincoln*, 227.
33. Lincoln, *Collected Works*, 2:248.
34. Ibid., 2:362.
35. Ibid., 2:467, original emphasis.
36. Ibid., 2:506.
37. Ibid., 3:20, 22, original emphasis.
38. Burlingame, *Abraham Lincoln*, 1:488; quoted in Burlingame, *Abraham Lincoln*, 1:488; Burlingame, *Abraham Lincoln*, 1:389–90; Stern, headnote, "From Lincoln's Opening Speech," 475.
39. Quoted in Burlingame, *Abraham Lincoln*, 1:534; quoted in Zall, *Abe Lincoln Laughing*, 5.

40. Brooks, "Personal Reminiscences," 562; Bray, "Power to Hurt," 57.
41. de Certeau, *Practice of Everyday Life*, 37.
42. McPherson, *Battle Cry of Freedom*, 267, 271, 255; Stampp, "Lincoln and the Secession Crisis," 75. Lincoln's intentions in this resupply effort have long been the source of contentious historical debate. McPherson, for one, thinks, "Although he never said explicitly what he expected them [the Confederates] to do, Lincoln had become rather disillusioned with the prospects for voluntary reconstruction and he had plenty of reason to believe that the Confederates would open fire on a peaceful resupply effort." *Battle Cry of Freedom*, 272n78. McPherson's note includes a useful synthesis of other major positions in this debate.
43. Browning, *Diary*, 1:476; Oliver Ellsworth to Lincoln, April 18, 1861, Abraham Lincoln Papers, original emphasis.
44. Hay, *Inside Lincoln's White House*, 103; Goodwin, *Team of Rivals*, 566; quoted in R. B. Browne, *Lincoln-Lore*, 94; Chase, *Salmon P. Chase Papers*, 180.

3. The Rail-Splitter President

1. F. F. Browne, *Every-Day Life*, 329.
2. Howe, *Making the American Self*, 136; Hofstadter, *American Political Tradition*, 93.
3. Cawelti, *Apostles*, 9. According to Cawelti, "in the dramatic story of Abraham Lincoln's rise from rail-splitter to President, from poverty and obscurity to savior of the union, the ideal of the self-made man found its greatest epic." *Apostles*, 40.
4. Lincoln, *Collected Works*, 1:8–9.
5. Cawelti, *Apostles*, 2.
6. Wilson and Davis, *Herndon's Informants*, 118, 104, 106–7; Logan, "Stephen T. Logan," 2; Wilson and Davis, *Herndon's Informants*, 106–7.
7. Winkle, *Young Eagle*, 74–75.
8. Plummer, *Lincoln's Rail-Splitter*, 42, 53; Harper, *Lincoln and the Press*, 49; Carwardine, *Lincoln*, 103. Douglas L. Wilson, in explaining Lincoln's intense privacy, claims, "Even though they [his advisers and publicists] had made it clear that his career had a rags-to-riches character that could be politically advantageous, he was unwilling to cooperate," and Wilson gives as evidence Lincoln's biographical apologia, "There is not much of it, for the reason, I suppose, that there is not much of me." *Lincoln's Sword*, 79. But, as argued in this chapter, Lincoln's apparent reluctance may have been in part a folksy but astute performance of modesty that mapped to circulating images of the self-made man. Carwardine offers a similar take: "Lincoln was entirely alert to the

political benefits of projecting his humble origins, but this did not mean that there was anything contrived about his interest in the common folk. He empathized with those who were, as he had been, struggling self-improvers." *Lincoln*, 50. For analysis of how the Republican Party continued to connect Lincoln's laboring past to a critique of slavery during Lincoln's presidency, see Richardson, *Greatest Nation of the Earth*.

9. Lincoln, *Collected Works*, 4:65, 62, 63. See also Burlingame, "Writing Lincoln's Lives"; Burlingame, *Abraham Lincoln* 1:648; and Sandburg, *Abraham Lincoln*, 120.

10. Howells, *Life of Abraham Lincoln*, 19–21.

11. Ibid., 47, 57.

12. Winkle, *Young Eagle*, 125.

13. Crockett, *Account*, 46–47. According to Richard Boyd Henry, this book is "factual, but not autobiographical—its first person narration is a sham. Here can be found the stories of Crockett's reception in the big cities, told in a style that is a Whig ghostwriter's imitation of Crockett's. The congressman's legend had preceded him, and Crockett played the role he believed was appropriate to his public image." "Man in the Buckskin Hunting Shirt," 11.

14. Crockett, *Narrative*, 16, original emphasis; Shackford, *David Crockett*, 12; Lincoln, *Collected Works*, 4:62.

15. Strange, *Sketches and Eccentricities*, 128.

16. Quoted in Lofaro, introduction, xxii, original emphasis.

17. Zall, *Abe Lincoln's Legacy*, xvi.

18. Casper, introduction, 9; Benson, *Printed Picture*, 22, 50; Winship, "Manufacturing and Book Production," 50. In lithography, artists drew directly onto a piece of limestone using a beeswax crayon; after being treated with acid, the composition was treated with ink and water and could be used to print many copies. Benson, *Printed Picture*, 50.

19. Benson, *Printed Picture*, 24; Winship, "Manufacturing and Book Production," 64; Press, *Political Cartoon*, 4; Barnhurst and Nerone, *Form of News*, 114.

20. Nerone, "Newspapers and the Public Sphere," 241–42; W. F. Thompson, *Image of War*, 169; Bunker, *From Rail-Splitter*, 31.

21. W. F. Thompson, *Image of War*, 167; Lively, "Propaganda Techniques," 101.

22. Bunker, *From Rail-Splitter*, 9.

23. Holzer, *Lincoln Seen and Heard*, 37.

24. "Tribune Offering," 73; Carwardine, *Lincoln*, 74; W. B. Brown, "Cincinnatus Image," 23, 26.

25. "Last Rail Split," 61; Carwardine, *Lincoln*, 104.

26. "Uncle Sam." Though scholars disagree on the exact origins of the Uncle Sam figure, it can likely be traced to the War of 1812, when Sam Wilson of Troy, New York, stamped barrels of meat to be sent to U.S. troops with "U.S."; his workers joked that it stood for "Uncle Sam" Wilson. The Uncle Sam figure first appeared in a lithograph in 1837; by 1860 it had not yet begun to morph with the bearded image of Lincoln, as it would later during the Civil War. Lordan, *Politics, Ink*, 119–20.
27. Bellew, "Lincoln's Last Warning," 61, original emphasis.
28. "Good Gracious, Abraham Lincoln!" 16; Lordan, *Politics, Ink*, 18.
29. Baker, "Rail Splitter at Work Repairing the Union."
30. "Job for the New Cabinet Maker," 5.
31. "Cooperation," 1.
32. *Workingman's Reasons*, 1–2, original emphasis.
33. Lowell, *Works*, 208.
34. Stowe, *Men of Our Times*, 13, original emphasis.
35. Hurz, "Log Cabin Built," 1.
36. Quoted in John L. Scripps to William H. Herndon, Chicago, June 24, 1865, in Wilson and Davis, *Herndon's Informants*, 57. Fehrenbacher and Fehrenbacher, *Recollected Words*, 395–96.

4. "Abraham Africanus the First": The Limits of Preemptive Self-Satire

1. Nast, "President Lincoln's Inaugural," 320.
2. Tebbel, *Media in America*, 189, 195–96. The term "Copperhead" is an epithet—in wide use by 1862—referring to Peace Democrats during the Civil War. Though Republicans used it because it described a poisonous snake, some Democrats embraced the term. A penny is also called a "copperhead," and Peace Democrats argued that because pennies then depicted Lady Liberty, Copperheads were resisting the president's assault on civil liberties and the Constitution. Weber, "Lincoln's Critics," 33.
3. Wyllie, *Self-Made Man in America*, 117; Alger, *Abraham Lincoln*, 78; Cawelti, *Apostles*, 2–3.
4. Norton, review, 4.
5. Fehrenbacher, "Anti-Lincoln Tradition," 8–9. See also Holzer, "Confederate Caricature," and Abbott, "President Lincoln," 307.
6. Quoted in Channing, *Crisis of Fear*, 230.
7. "Masks and Faces," 8. For more on *Southern Illustrated News*, see Holzer, "Confederate Caricature," 28.
8. Volck, "Lincoln Signing."
9. "Abduction," 4; Holzer, "Confederate Caricature," 28; "Southern Punch," n.p.

10. *Lincoln Catechism*, 3; *Abraham Africanus I*, 9, 41, 26–27, 31, 6–7, 20, 22, original emphasis.
11. Freedberg, *Power of Images*, 257.
12. Lincoln, *Collected Works*, 3:535–36, 538.
13. Quoted in Fite, *Presidential Campaign of 1860*, 210.
14. Adderup, *Lincolniana*, 8.
15. G. W. Harris, *Sut Lovingood Travels*, 21–22, 28, 35–36.
16. Hall, *Reflections*, 3; C. H. Smith, *Bill Arp*, 24; Lincoln, *Collected Works*, 2:498.
17. *God Bless Abraham Lincoln*, 4, 14.
18. See M. T. Smith, "Beast Unleashed," 248–76.
19. *God Bless Abraham Lincoln*, 14–16.
20. Adderup, *Lincolniana*, back matter; *Lincoln Catechism*, 3–5, 12, 37.
21. *Lincoln Catechism*, 38.
22. *God Bless Abraham Lincoln*, 15.
23. Strother, Lincoln as monkey. Holzer assesses Confederate caricature in illustrated weeklies and vanity presses, "At best, they were crudely drawn and uninventive. At worst, they were so bitter that they went beyond satire; they became merely illustrated invective." "Confederate Caricature," 29. I agree with this evaluation and would extend it to written satires, as well.
24. Holzer, Boritt, and Neely, *Lincoln Image*, 116, 126–27; Neely, Holzer, and Boritt, *Confederate Image*, 51. These authors offer a useful comparison of influence of Adalbert Volck and Thomas Nast: "Whereas Nast's sketches were regularly engraved for the popular Northern weeklies, Volck's works enjoyed no comparable mass circulation, and as far as is known, no circulation in the Confederacy until the war was over." Neely, Holzer, and Boritt, *Confederate Image*, 44. Incidentally, Volck seems to have at least partially recanted his anti-Lincoln illustrations. In a 1905 letter to the Library of Congress, he says that he felt "the greatest regret ever to have aimed ridicule at that good and great Lincoln," though, as Neely, Holzer, and Boritt note, in the same letter he also says, "Outside of that the pictures represent events as truthfully as my close connections with the South enabled me to get at them." He later presented a carved shield to the Confederate Museum in Richmond in 1909, so the sincerity of his apology is debatable. *Confederate Image*, 54.
25. Holzer, *Mirror Image*, 24; Tebbel, *Media in America*, 184; Holzer, "Confederate Caricature," 24, 26.
26. Quoted in Christie, "Civil War Humor," 103; C. H. Smith, *Bill Arp*, 5–6.
27. Abbott, "President Lincoln," 314.
28. Adderup, *Lincolniana*, back matter.

29. Plummer, *Lincoln's Rail-Splitter*, 52.
30. As Jane W. Stedman relates, the humor periodical London *Punch's* "greatest source of language humor was American English, which *Punch's* editors regarded as a different and subversive tongue." "American English," 171–72.
31. "President Lincoln's Inaugural Speech," 237.
32. "The War in America," *Comic News*, July 23, 1864, 29, and August 27, 1864, 93, quoted in Bunker, "*Comic News*," 64.
33. Tenniel, "Great 'Cannon Game,'" 191, original emphasis.
34. *Old Abe's Jokes*, 28–29.
35. Lowell, *Works*, 192.
36. Bunker, *Rail-Splitter*, 3.
37. Morgan, "Pull Devil—Pull Baker," 159.
38. Morgan, "Vampire," 221; Morgan, "In for His Second Innings," 240.
39. Maurer, "Punch," 4, 27, 28.
40. Neely, Holzer, and. Boritt, *Confederate Image*, 5; Bunker, "*Comic News*," 54; quoted in Russell, *My Diary*, 401.
41. Bunker, "*Comic News*," 87; Morgan, *American War*, n.p.
42. Tenniel, "Britannia Sympathises with Columbia," 183. According to Tenniel's *New York Times* obituary of February 27, 1914, under the headline "Tenniel, Cartoonist, Dead: Famous Punch Artist, Who Caricatured Lincoln, Was Aged 94," Shirley Brooks wrote the poem. According to Holzer, the poem was written by Tom Taylor, who wrote the play that Lincoln was watching when he was shot. Holzer, *Lincoln Seen*, 125.
43. "Abraham Lincoln, Foully Assassinated," 2.

5. *"A Hoosier Michael Angelo": The Politics of Lincoln's Physical Appearance in Popular Media*

1. Carpenter, *Six Months*, 148–49; Zall, *Abe Lincoln's Legacy*, 57.
2. Pratt, *Concerning Mr. Lincoln*, 19–20.
3. Two important exceptions include Harold Holzer and Gary L. Bunker. Holzer complains of a critical legacy that continually sees "Lincoln as the undeserving victim of the most brutal pictorial assault in the long history of relationships between artists and leaders." He offers several commonsense correctives, including his observations that Lincoln was the leading cartoon target of the time precisely because he was its "leading personality" and that "he was treated no more harshly than any of his rivals for the presidency, nor as brutally during his term of office than any previous, controversial occupant of the White House." *Lincoln Seen*, 105–6. In historicizing the new maturity of the illustrated comic periodical in 1860, Bunker asserts the centrality of political cartoons

to Lincoln's electoral successes: "This new watershed of political caricature was fortuitous for Abraham Lincoln, for it helped to transform his status from dark horse candidate to president of the United States." *From Rail-Splitter*, 31.

4. Carwardine, *Lincoln*, 50. Michael Woods discusses Lincoln's physical regularities while speculating as to whether he may have had the genetic disorder Marfan syndrome. "Lincoln's Health Draws Scrutiny," 25. But several experts have considered and dismissed this possibility. See, for instance, Boritt and Borit, "Lincoln and the Marfan Syndrome," and Lattimer, "Danger in Claiming."

5. *Only Authentic Life*, 1, 14.

6. *Democratic Campaign Songster*, 12, 4.

7. Whitman, "Walt Whitman," 82.

8. Whipple, *Story-Life of Lincoln*, 316; Norman B. Judd to Abraham Lincoln, June 6, 1860, Abraham Lincoln Papers.

9. Holzer, Borritt, and Neely, *Lincoln Image*, 67; Horan, *Mathew Brady*, 31. One scholar of photography explains the power of this photograph: "Most people had never seen Lincoln, but rumors of his ugliness were rife during the presidential campaign. . . . Brady distracted attention from Lincoln's gangliness by directing light to his face. He posed the future president in a statesmanlike attitude and took care that he curled his fingers (especially of his right hand), so that they would not appear overly long and large." Marien, *Photography*, 95.

10. "Editor's Drawer," 1866, 405.

11. Quoted in Carwardine, *Lincoln*, 72; Burlingame, *Abraham Lincoln*, 1:657–58.

12. Lincoln, *Collected Works*, 3:512. Other scholars have mentioned Lincoln's strategic self-mockery. Benjamin Thomas comments, "He had no illusions about his personal appearance and joked about it so often that there is reason to believe that he deliberately tried to capitalize upon his homeliness." *"Lincoln's Humor,"* 12. Carwardine maintains, "Lincoln certainly described himself as ugly and used his appearance as a weapon against himself, for humorous effect." *Lincoln*, 50.

13. Carwardine, *Lincoln*, 50–51; Conwell, *Why Lincoln Laughed*, 21. Lincoln had a "new suit of clothes" for the Cooper Union speech, but it "had become badly creased from packing." Stern, headnote, "Address," 568–69.

14. *Only Authentic Life*, 14–15.

15. Holzer, Boritt, and Neely, *Lincoln Image*, xviii.

16. Huntzicker, *Popular Press*, 108; Brooks, "Personal Reminiscences of Lincoln," 15.4:562.

17. Bartlett, *Life and Public Services*, 107.

18. Quoted in Holzer, *Lincoln Seen*, 128, 107.
19. Harrison, *Cartoon*, 68.
20. Holzer cautions about reading too far into Lincoln's attitudes about political cartoons: "We have no idea how Lincoln reacted to humorous prints. . . . Nor is there any surviving evidence of how fellow Americans of Lincoln's era responded to these pictures. The galling absence of such documentation makes any examination of their impact on the Lincoln image at best speculative." *Lincoln Seen*, 104.
21. Lincoln, *Collected Works*, 2:149–50. Earlier in the speech, Lincoln had set up this punch line by referring to a "biographical sketch" of Pierce "in which he is represented, at the age of seventeen, to have spelled 'but' for his father, who was unable to spell it for himself" and in which a U.S.-Mexico War story was told picturing Pierce "as cutting at the enemy's flying cannon balls with his sword in the battles of Mexico, and calling out, 'Boys there's a game of ball for you;' and finally that he added enough to a balance due him to raise the whole to three hundred dollars, and treated his men." *Collected Works*, 2:148.
22. Bellew, "'A Rail' Old Western Gentleman," 14–15; quoted in Plummer, *Lincoln's Rail-Splitter*, 52.
23. A. Johnson, *Stephen A. Douglas*, 364–65; quoted in Plummer, *Lincoln's Rail-Splitter*, 53.
24. Lincoln, *Collected Works*, 2:506.
25. "Honest Old Abe," 1; West, *"Phunny Phellow,"* n.p.
26. Benedict, *"Wide Awake" Poem*, 8, 10, original emphasis.
27. "'Boy' Lost!"
28. Burlingame, *Abraham Lincoln*, 1:249; quoted in J. K. Morehead, interview with John G. Nicolay, May 12 and 13, 1880, in Burlingame, *Oral History*, 41.
29. Cohen, "Manly Sport," n.p.; "Political Race." Bunker lists numerous 1860 cartoons showing Douglas as embattled and Lincoln as capturing initiative. *From Rail-Splitter*, 66.
30. "Lincoln, Douglas, and the Rail-Fence Handicap"; Cohen, "Manly Sport," n.p.
31. Harrison, *Cartoon*, 61.
32. Dawley, *President Lincoln Campaign Songster*, 14; Nast, "May the Best Man Win," 8–9.
33. Bunker states that in 1864 "the visual and verbal creations of illustrated periodicals were integral parts of Lincoln's political machine." *From Rail-Splitter*, 322–23.
34. Bellew, "Presidential Cobblers and Wire-Pullers," 297.

35. "May the Best Man Win," 8–9; Bellew, "Good Uncle and the Naughty Boy," 16.
36. W. F. Thompson, *Image of War*, 174; Bellew, "This Reminds Me," 608.
37. Bellew, "Long Abraham Lincoln," 768; Press, *Political Cartoon*, 19.
38. "With All Thy Faults," 8–9.
39. "Jeff Davis's November Nightmare," 176.
40. Newman, "Tallest Ruler on the Globe." See also Bunker, "Old Abe," 37–41.
41. Newman, "Phenomenon of Portraiture," 8.
42. Streicher, "On a Theory," 440.
43. Ward, "A. Ward, Jr. on the Presidency," 1. On the importance of small-town papers supporting Lincoln in 1864, see Carwardine, *Lincoln*, 295.

Bibliography

Abbott, Martin. "President Lincoln in Confederate Caricature." *Journal of the Illinois State Historical Society* 51.3 (1958): 306–20.

"Abduction of the Yankee Goddess of Liberty." Cartoon. *Southern Punch*, November 4, 1863, 4.

Abraham Africanus I: His Secret Life, Revealed under the Mesmeric Influence, Mysteries of the White House. New York: Feeks, 1864.

"Abraham Lincoln. Foully Assassinated, April 14, 1865." *Frank Leslie's Budget of Fun*, July 1865, 2.

Adderup, Andrew. *Lincolniana, or Humors of Uncle Abe.* New York: Feeks, 1864.

Alger, Horatio, Jr. *Abraham Lincoln, the Young Backwoods Boy, or How a Young Rail Splitter Became President.* New York: Anderson and Allen, 1883.

Arp, Bill. *See* Smith, Charles H.

Baker, Joseph E. "Columbia Demands Her Children!" Cartoon. Boston, 1864. http://www.loc.gov/pictures/item/2008661676/.

———. "The Rail Splitter at Work Repairing the Union." Cartoon. New York: Currier and Ives, July 1865. loc.gov/item/scsm000387/.

Bakhtin, Mikhail. *Problems of Dostoevsky's Poetics.* Edited and translated by Caryl Emerson. Minneapolis: University of Minnesota Press, 1984.

———. *Rabelais and His World.* Translated by Hellene Iswolsky. Cambridge, MA: MIT Press, 1968.

Barnhurst, Kevin G., and John Nerone. *The Form of the News: A History.* New York: Guilford, 2001.

Bartlett, David W. *The Life and Public Services of Hon. Abraham Lincoln.* New York: Broaders, 1860.

Bellew, Frank. "The Good Uncle and the Naughty Boy." Cartoon. *Frank Leslie's Budget of Fun*, December 1, 1864, 16.

———. "Lincoln's Last Warning." Cartoon. *Harper's Weekly*, October 11, 1862, 61.

———. "Long Abraham Lincoln a Little Longer." Cartoon. *Harper's Weekly*, November 26, 1864, 768.

———. "The National Joker." Cartoon. *Funniest of Phun*, September 1864, 16.

———. "Presidential Cobblers and Wire-Pullers Measuring and Estimating Lincoln's Shoes." Cartoon. *New York Illustrated News*, March 5, 1864, 297.

———. "'A Rail' Old Western Gentleman." In R. R. Wilson, *Lincoln in Caricature*, 14–15.

———. "This Reminds Me of a Little Joke." Cartoon. *Harper's Weekly*, September 17, 1864, 608.

Benedict, Almon. *A "Wide Awake" Poem*. Cortland Village, NY: Van Slyck, 1860.

Benson, Richard. *The Printed Picture*. New York: Museum of Modern Art, 2008.

Berkelman, Robert. "Lincoln's Interest in Shakespeare." *Shakespeare Quarterly* 2.4 (1951): 303–12.

Blair, Montgomery. Manuscripts, 1843–81. Lilly Library, Indiana University, Bloomington, Indiana.

Blair, Walter. *Horse Sense in American Humor: From Benjamin Franklin to Ogden Nash*. Chicago: University of Chicago Press, 1942.

———. *Native American Humor (1800–1900)*. New York: American Book, 1937.

Blegen, Theodore. *Lincoln's Imagery: A Study in Word Power*. La Crosse, WI: Sumac, 1954.

Boritt, Gabor S. "Punch Lincoln: Some Thoughts on Cartoons in the British Magazine." *Journal of the Abraham Lincoln Association* 15.1 (1994): 1–21.

Boritt, Gabor S., and Adam Borit. "Lincoln and the Marfan Syndrome: The Medical Diagnosis of a Historical Figure." *Civil War History* 29.3 (1983): 212–29.

"'Boy' Lost!" Broadside. 1860. Lilly Library, Indiana University, Bloomington, Indiana.

Bray, Robert. "'The Power to Hurt': Lincoln's Early Use of Satire and Invective." *Journal of the Abraham Lincoln Association* 16.1 (1995): 39–58.

———. *Reading with Lincoln*. Carbondale: Southern Illinois University Press, 2010.

———. "What Abraham Lincoln Read: An Evaluative and Annotated List." *Journal of the Abraham Lincoln Association* 28.2 (2007): 28–81.

Brooks, Noah. "Personal Reminiscences of Lincoln." *Scribner's Monthly* 15.4, 1878, 561–69.

———. "Personal Reminiscences of Lincoln." *Scribner's Monthly* 15.5, 1878, 673–81.

Brown, W. Burlie. "The Cincinnatus Image in Presidential Politics." *Agricultural History* 31.1 (1957): 22–39.

Browne, Francis Fisher. *The Every-Day Life of Abraham Lincoln.* 1887. Edited by John Y. Simon. Lincoln: University of Nebraska Press, 1995.

Browne, Ray B., ed. *Lincoln-Lore: Lincoln in the Popular Mind.* Bowling Green, OH: Popular, 1974.

Browning, Orville Hickman. *The Diary of Orville Hickman Browning.* Springfield: Illinois State Library, 1925.

Bunker, Gary L. "The *Comic News,* Lincoln, and the Civil War." *Journal of the Abraham Lincoln Association* 17.1 (1996): 53–87.

———. *From Rail-Splitter to Icon: Lincoln's Image in Illustrated Periodicals, 1860–1865.* Kent: Kent State University Press, 2001.

———. "'Old Abe' in Political Caricature: Revisiting the Drawn Lincoln." *OAH Magazine of History* 23.1 (2009): 37–46.

Burke, Kenneth. *A Grammar of Motives.* New York: Braziller, 1955.

———. "Why Satire, with a Plan for Writing One." *Michigan Quarterly Review* 13 (1974): 307–37.

Burlingame, Michael. *Abraham Lincoln: A Life.* 2 vols. Baltimore: Johns Hopkins University Press, 2008.

———. *The Inner World of Abraham Lincoln.* Urbana: University of Illinois Press, 1994.

———, ed. *An Oral History of Abraham Lincoln: John G. Nicolay's Interviews and Essays.* Carbondale: Southern Illinois University Press, 1996.

———. "Writing Lincoln's Lives." Multimedia. Excerpt from *Abraham Lincoln: A Life,* 2008. *Journal Divided,* October 2010. housedivided.dickinson.edu /sites/journal/2010/10/14/writing-lincolns-lives/.

Burt, Silas W. "Lincoln on His Own Story-Telling." *Century Illustrated Monthly Magazine,* 1907, 502.

Caron, James E. "Backwoods Civility, or How the Ring-Tailed Roarer Became a Gentle Man for David Crockett, Charles F. M. Noland, and William Tappan Thompson." In Inge and Piacentino, *Humor of the Old South,* 161–86.

Carpenter, Francis. "Anecdotes and Reminiscences of Abraham Lincoln." In *The Life and Public Services of Abraham Lincoln,* edited by Henry J. Raymond, 753–54. New York: Derby and Miller, 1865.

———. *Six Months at the White House with Abraham Lincoln.* New York: Hurd and Houghton, 1866.

Carwardine, Richard. *Lincoln: A Life of Purpose and Power.* New York: Vintage, 2007.

Casper, Scott E. Introduction. In Casper, Groves, Nissenbaum, and Winship, *History of the Book,* 1–39.

Casper, Scott. E., Jeffrey D. Groves, Stephen W. Nissenbaum, and Michael Winship, eds. *A History of the Book in America; Vol. 3: The Industrial Book 1840–1880*. Chapel Hill: University of North Carolina Press, 2007.

Cawelti, John G. *Apostles of the Self-Made Man*. Chicago: University of Chicago Press, 1965.

Channing, Steven A. *Crisis of Fear: Secession in South Carolina*. New York: Norton, 1974.

Chase, Salmon P. *The Salmon P. Chase Papers: Correspondence, April 1863–1864*. Edited by John Niven. Kent: Kent State University Press, 1997.

Christie, Anne M. "Civil War Humor: Bill Arp." *Civil War History* 2.3 (1956): 103–19.

Cohen, Kenneth. "The Manly Sport of American Politics: Or, How We Came to Call Elections 'Races.'" *Common-Place* 12.3 (2012). common-place.org.

Conwell, Russell H. *Why Lincoln Laughed*. New York: Harper and Brothers, 1922.

Cook, Sylvia J. "Camp Meetings, Comedy, and Erskine Caldwell: From the Preposterous to the Absurd." In Piacentino, *Enduring Legacy*, 52–72.

"Cooperation." Cartoon. *Vanity Fair*, April 12, 1862, cover.

Crockett, David. *An Account of Col. Crockett's Tour to the North and Down East*. Philadelphia: Carey and Hart, 1835.

———. *An Autobiography of Davy Crockett*. Edited by Stephen Brennan. New York: Skyhorse, 2011.

———. *A Narrative of the Life of David Crockett*. Philadelphia: Hart, 1834.

"Crooked." *Frank Leslie's Illustrated Newspaper*, November 15, 1856, 355.

Dahlgren, Madeleine Vinton. *Memoir of John A. Dahlgren, Rear-Admiral United States Navy*. Boston: Osgood, 1882.

Dawley, T. R. *President Lincoln Campaign Songster*. Pamphlet. 1864. Lilly Library, Indiana University, Bloomington, Indiana.

de Certeau, Michel. *The Practice of Everyday Life*. Translated by Steven Randall. Berkeley: University of California Press, 1988.

The Democratic Campaign Songster. Cincinnati: American, 1860.

Depew, Chauncey M. "Chauncey M. Depew." In Rice, *Reminiscences*, 427–38.

Doig, Ivan. "The Genial White House Host and Raconteur." *Illinois State Historical Journal* 62 (1969): 307–11.

"Editor's Drawer." *Harper's Monthly* 32, February 1866, 405.

"Editor's Drawer." *Harper's New Monthly Magazine* 36, 1867, 537–38.

Elliott, Robert C. *The Power of Satire: Magic, Ritual, and Art*. Princeton: Princeton University Press, 1960.

Emerson, Ralph Waldo. "A Plain Man of the People." In *Building the Myth: Selected Speeches Memorializing Abraham Lincoln*, edited by Waldo Braden, 29–34. Urbana: University of Illinois Press, 1990.

"English Satire." *Knickerbocker Monthly* 61.1, 1863, 1.

Fehrenbacher, Don E. "The Anti-Lincoln Tradition." *Papers of the Abraham Lincoln Association* 4 (1982): 6–28.

Fehrenbacher, Don, and Virginia Fehrenbacher, eds. *Recollected Words of Abraham Lincoln.* Stanford: Stanford University Press, 1996.

Fite, Emerson David. *The Presidential Campaign of 1860.* New York: Macmillan, 1911.

Ford, Thomas. *A History of Illinois.* New York: Ivison and Phinny, 1854.

"Frank Leslie to the Budgetarians." *Frank Leslie's Budget of Fun,* November 1861, 1.

Freedberg, David. *The Power of Images: Studies in the History and Theory of Response.* Chicago: University of Chicago Press, 1989.

Frye, Northrop. *Anatomy of Criticism: Four Essays.* Princeton: Princeton University Press, 1957.

God Bless Abraham Lincoln: A Solemn Discourse by a Local Preacher. Pamphlet. N.p., 1862. Lilly Library, Indiana University, Bloomington, Indiana.

"Good Gracious, Abraham Lincoln!" Cartoon. *Frank Leslie's Budget of Fun,* January 1861, 16.

Goodwin, Doris Kearns. *Team of Rivals: The Political Genius of Abraham Lincoln.* New York: Simon and Schuster, 2005.

"Great and Astonishing Trick of Old Abe, the Western Juggler." Cartoon. *Frank Leslie's Budget of Fun,* April 15, 1861, 16.

Greenblatt, Stephen. *Renaissance Self-Fashioning from Moore to Shakespeare.* Chicago: University of Chicago Press, 1980.

Griffin, Dustin. *Satire: A Critical Reintroduction.* Lexington: University of Kentucky Press, 1994.

Hall, Wade D. *Reflections of the Civil War in Southern Humor.* Gainesville: University of Florida Press, 1962.

Halpine, Graham [Miles O'Reilly, pseud.]. *The Life and Adventures, Songs, Services, and Speeches of Private Miles O'Reilly.* New York: Carleton, 1864.

Hambrecht, George Philip. Manuscripts, 1860–1940. Lilly Library, Indiana University, Bloomington, Indiana.

Hanna, William F. *Abraham among the Yankees: Abraham Lincoln's 1848 Visit to Massachusetts.* Taunton, MA: Old Colony Historical Society, 1983.

Hannay, James. *Satire and Satirists.* New York: Redfield, 1855.

Harper, Robert S. *Lincoln and the Press.* New York: McGraw-Hill, 1951.

Harris, George Washington [Sut Lovingood]. *Sut Lovingood Travels with Old Abe Lincoln.* Chicago: Black Cat, 1942.

———. *Sut Lovingood: Yarns Spun by a Nat'ral Born Durn'd Fool.* New York: Dick and Fitzgerald, 1867.

Harris, Joel Chandler. "Humor in America." In *Critical Essays on American Humor,* edited by William Bedford Clark and W. Craig Turner, 46–49. Boston: Hall, 1984.

Harrison, Randall P. *The Cartoon: Communication to the Quick*. Beverly Hills: Sage, 1981.

Hay, John. *At Lincoln's Side: John Hay's Civil War Correspondence*. Edited by Michael Burlingame. Carbondale: Southern Illinois University Press, 2000.

———. *Inside Lincoln's White House: The Complete Civil War Diary of John Hay*. Edited by Michael Burlingame and John R. Turner Ettlinger. Carbondale: Southern Illinois University Press, 1997.

Henry, Richard Boyd. "The Man in the Buckskin Hunting Shirt." In *Davy Crockett: The Man, the Legend, the Legacy 1786–1986*, edited by Michael A. Lofaro, 3–20. Knoxville: University of Tennessee Press, 1985.

Herndon, William H., and Jesse William Weik. *Herndon's Lincoln*. Edited by Douglas L. Wilson and Rodney O. Davis. Urbana: Knox College Lincoln Studies Center, 2006.

"Hey, Uncle Abe, Are You Joking Yet?" Song sheet. New York: Feeks, 1864.

Highet, Gilbert. *The Anatomy of Satire*. Princeton: Princeton University Press, 1962.

Hofstadter, Richard. *The American Political Tradition and the Men Who Made It*. New York: Knopf, 1967.

Holzer, Harold. "The Campaign of 1860: Cooper Union, Mathew Brady, and the Campaign of Words and Images." In *Lincoln Revisited: New Insights from the Lincoln Forum*, edited by John Y. Simon, Harold Holzer, and Dawn Vogel, 57–80. New York: Fordham University Press, 2007.

———. "Confederate Caricature of Abraham Lincoln." *Illinois Historical Register* 80.1 (1987): 23–36.

———. *Lincoln Seen and Heard*. Lawrence: University of Kansas Press, 2000.

———. *The Mirror Image of Civil War Memory: Abraham Lincoln and Jefferson Davis in Popular Prints*. Fort Wayne, IN: Lincoln Museum, 1996.

Holzer, Harold, Gabor S. Boritt, and Mark E. Neely Jr. *The Lincoln Image: Abraham Lincoln and the Popular Print*. Urbana: University of Illinois Press, 2001.

"Honest Old Abe and the Little Boy in Search of His Mother—A Sensation Story." Cartoon. *Phunny Phellow*, November 1860, 1.

Horan, James D. *Mathew Brady: Historian with a Camera*. New York: Bonanza, 1955.

Howard, J. H. "I Knew Him, Horatio." Poster cartoon. New York: Strong, 1864.

Howe, Daniel Walker. *Making the American Self: Jonathan Edwards to Abraham Lincoln*. Cambridge, MA: Harvard University Press, 1997.

Howells, W. D. *The Life of Abraham Lincoln*. 1860. Bloomington: Indiana University Press, 1960.

"Humors of the Day." *Harper's Weekly*, June 1, 1861, 339.

Huntzicker, William E. *The Popular Press, 1833–1865*. Westport, CT: Greenwood, 1999.

Hurz, L. "Log Cabin Built by President Lincoln in Kentucky." Cartoon. *Frank Leslie's Illustrated Newspaper,* July 8, 1865, 1.

Inge, M. Thomas, and Edward Piacentino. *The Humor of the Old South.* Lexington: University Press of Kentucky, 2001.

Jameson, Fredric. *Fables of Aggression.* Berkeley: University of California Press, 1979.

"Jeff Davis's November Nightmare." Cartoon. *Frank Leslie's Illustrated Newspaper,* December 3, 1864, 176.

Jennison, Keith W. *The Humorous Mr. Lincoln: A Profile in Wit, Courage, and Compassion.* Woodstock, VT: Countryman, 2002.

"A Job for the New Cabinet Maker." Cartoon. *Frank Leslie's Illustrated Newspaper,* February 2, 1861, 5.

Johannsen, Robert W. "Stephen A. Douglas' New England Campaign, 1860." *New England Quarterly* 35 (1962): 162–86.

Johnson, Allen. *Stephen A. Douglas: A Study in American Politics.* 1908. New York: De Capo, 1970.

Johnson, Julie Greer. *Satire in Colonial Spanish America: Turning the World Upside Down.* Austin: University of Texas Press, 1993.

Justus, James H. *Fetching the Old Southwest: Humorous Writing from Longstreet to Twain.* Columbia: University of Missouri Press, 2004.

———. Introduction. In Inge and Piacentino, *Humor of the Old South,* 1–12.

Kaplan, Fred. *Lincoln: The Biography of a Writer.* New York: HarperCollins, 2008.

Klunder, Willard Carl. *Lewis Cass and the Politics of Moderation.* Kent: Kent State University Press, 1996.

"The Last Rail Split by 'Honest Old Abe.'" Cartoon. *Momus,* June 2, 1860, 61.

Lattimer, John K. "The Danger in Claiming that Abraham Lincoln Had the Marfan Syndrome." *Lincoln Fellowship of Wisconsin Historical Bulletin* 46 (1991): 38–47.

———. "Lincoln Did Not Have the Marfan Syndrome." *New York State Journal of Medicine* (1981): 1805–13.

Lentricchia, Frank. *Criticism and Social Change.* Chicago: University of Chicago Press, 1983.

Lincoln, Abraham. Abraham Lincoln Papers at the Library of Congress. Manuscript Division. American Memory Project, 2000–2002. Washington, DC. http://memory.loc.gov/ammem/alhtml/alhome.html. Accessed February 16, 2014.

———. *The Collected Works of Abraham Lincoln.* 8 vols. Edited by Roy P. Basler. New Brunswick: Rutgers University Press, 1953.

———. *The Life and Writings of Abraham Lincoln.* Edited by Philip Van Doren Stern. New York: Modern Library, 2000.

———. *Mr. Lincoln's Funnybone: Wherein the White House Joker Retells His Best Yarns & Fables.* Edited by Loyd Dunning. New York: Howell, Soskin, 1942.

The Lincoln Catechism, Wherein the Eccentricities and Beauties of Despotism Are Fully Set Forth: A Guide to the Presidential Election of 1864. New York: Feeks, 1864.

"Lincoln, Douglas, and the Rail-Fence Handicap." Poster cartoon. Buffalo, New York, July 1860.

Lively, James K. "Propaganda Techniques of Civil War Cartoonists." *Public Opinion Quarterly* 6 (1942): 99–106.

Lofaro, Michael A. *The Tall Tales of Davy Crockett: The Second Nashville Series of Crockett Almanacs 1839–1841.* Knoxville: University of Tennessee Press, 1987.

Logan, Stephen T. "Stephen T. Logan Talks about Lincoln." *Bulletin of the Lincoln Centennial Association* 12.1 (1928): 1–5.

Lordan, Edward J. *Politics, Ink: How America's Cartoonists Skewer Politicians, from King George III to George Dubya.* New York: Rowman and Littlefield, 2006.

Lovingood, Sut. *See* Harris, George Washington.

Lowell, James Russell. *The Works of James Russell Lowell.* Vol. 5. Cambridge, MA: Riverside, 1890.

Luthin, Reinard. "Abraham Lincoln and the Massachusetts Whigs in 1848." *New England Quarterly* 14 (1941): 619–32.

Marien, Mary Warner. *Photography: A Cultural History.* London: King, 2002.

"Masks and Faces." Cartoon. *Southern Illustrated News,* November 8, 1862, 8.

Maurer, Oscar. "'Punch' on Slavery and the Civil War in America, 1841–1865." *Victorian Studies* 1.1 (1957): 4–28.

McGill, Meredith L. *American Literature and the Culture of Reprinting.* Philadelphia: University of Pennsylvania Press, 2003.

McPherson, James. *Battle Cry of Freedom: The Civil War Era.* Oxford: Oxford University Press, 1988.

———. "How Lincoln Won the War with Metaphor." In *With My Face to the Enemy: Perspectives on the Civil War,* edited by Robert Crowley, 87–102. New York: Putnam's Sons, 2001.

Minier, George W. "Geo. W. Minier." In *The Lincoln Memorial: Album-Immortelles,* edited by Osborn H. Oldroyd, 187–90. Chicago: GEM, 1882.

Mitgang, Herbert, ed. *Abraham Lincoln: A Press Portrait.* Athens: University of Georgia Press, 1989.

Morgan, Matthew Somerville. *The American War.* London: Chatto and Windus, 1874.

———. "In for His Second Innings." Cartoon. *Comic News,* December 6, 1864, 240.

———. "Pull Devil—Pull Baker." Cartoon. *Comic News,* October 8, 1864, 159.

———. "The Vampire." Cartoon. *Comic News*, November 26, 1864, 221.

Nast, Thomas. "May the Best Man Win—Uncle Sam Reviewing the Army of Candidates for the Presidential Chair." Cartoon. *Phunny Phellow*, April 1864, 8–9.

———. "President's Lincoln's Inaugural." Cartoon. *New York Illustrated News*, March 23, 1861, 320.

Neely, Mark E., Jr. *The Boundaries of American Political Culture in the Civil War Era*. Chapel Hill: University of North Carolina Press, 2005.

Neely, Mark E., Jr., Harold Holzer, and Gabor S. Boritt. *The Confederate Image: Prints of the Lost Cause*. Chapel Hill: University of North Carolina Press, 1987.

Nerone, John. "Newspapers and the Public Sphere." In Casper, Groves, Nissenbaum, and Winship, *History of the Book*, 230–47.

Newman, William. "A Phenomenon of Portraiture." Cartoon. *Frank Leslie's Budget of Fun*, December 15, 1860, 8.

———. "The Tallest Ruler on the Globe." Cartoon. *Frank Leslie's Budget of Fun*, April 1865.

Nicolay, Helen. *Personal Traits of Abraham Lincoln*. New York: Century, 1912.

Norton, Charles Eliot. Review of *History of the Administration of President Lincoln*. By Henry J. Raymond. *North American Review* 100.206 (1865): 1–20.

Old Abe's Joker, or Wit at the White House. New York: Wehman, 1863.

Old Abe's Jokes, Fresh from Abraham's Bosom, Containing All His Issue, Excepting the "Greenbacks," to Call in Some of Which, This Work Is Issued. New York: Dawley, 1864.

The Only Authentic Life of Abraham Lincoln, Alias "Old Abe," a Son of the West: With an Account of His Birth and Education, His Rail-Splitting and Flat-Boating, His Joke-Cutting and Soldiering, with Some Allusions to His Journeys from Springfield to Washington and Back Again. New York: Offices of *Comic Monthly*, 1864.

O'Reilly, Miles. *See* Halpine, Graham.

Palmeri, Frank. *Satire in Narrative*. Austin: University of Texas Press, 1990.

Paxton, Philip. *A Stray Yankee in Texas*. New York: Redfield, 1853.

Piacentino, Ed, ed. *The Enduring Legacy of Old Southwest Humor*. Baton Rouge: Louisiana State University Press, 2006.

———. "Intersecting Paths: The Humor of the Old Southwest as Intertext." In Piacentino, *Enduring Legacy*, 1–35.

Plummer, Mark A. *Lincoln's Rail-Splitter: Governor Richard J. Oglesby*. Urbana: University of Illinois Press, 2001.

"A Political Race." Poster cartoon. New York: Rickey, Mallory, September 1860.

"Political Satire and Satirists." *United States Magazine, and Democratic Review* 11.54 (1842): 621–30.

Poore, Benjamin Perley. "Benjamin Perley Poore." In Rice, *Reminiscences*, 217–31.

Pratt, Harry E., comp. *Concerning Mr. Lincoln, in Which Abraham Lincoln Is Pictured as He Appeared to Letter Writers of His Time*. Springfield, IL: Abraham Lincoln Association, 1944.

"The President and the Office-Seekers." *Frank Leslie's Illustrated Newspaper*, October 31, 1863, 87.

"President Lincoln's Inaugural Speech." *Punch* (London), December 10, 1864, 237.

Press, Charles. *The Political Cartoon*. Rutherford: Fairleigh Dickinson University Press, 1981.

Raymond, Henry J. *The Life and Public Services of Abraham Lincoln, Sixteenth President of the United States; Together with His State Papers, Including His Speeches, Addresses, Messages, Letters, and Proclamations, and the Closing Scenes Connected with His Life and Death*. New York: Darby and Miller, 1865.

"Reprinted Letter." *Frank Leslie's Budget of Fun*, May 1, 1861, 2.

Reynolds, David S. *Beneath the American Renaissance*. Cambridge, MA: Harvard University Press, 1989.

Rice, Allen Thorndike, ed. *Reminiscences of Abraham Lincoln by Distinguished Men of His Time*. New York: North American, 1886.

Richardson, Heather Cox. *The Greatest Nation of the Earth: Republican Economic Policies during the Civil War*. Cambridge, MA: Harvard University Press, 1997.

Rosenheim, Edward, Jr. "Norms, Moral and Other, in Satire: A Symposium." *Satire Newsletter* 2.1 (1964): 2–25.

Rourke, Constance. *American Humor: A Study of the National Character*. New York: Harcourt, 1931.

Rugg, Arthur Prentice. *Abraham Lincoln in Worcester*. Worcester, MA: Belisle, 1914.

Russell, William Howard. *My Diary North and South*. New York: Harper, 1863.

Sandage, Scott A. *Born Losers: A History of Failure in America*. Cambridge, MA: Harvard University Press, 2005.

Sandburg, Carl. *Abraham Lincoln: The Prairie Years and the War Years*. New York: Harcourt, 1939.

Schutz, Charles E. *Political Humor: From Aristophanes to Sam Ervin*. Rutherford: Fairleigh Dickinson University Press, 1977.

Scott, John M., to Ida Tarbell, Bloomington, Illinois, August 14, 1895. Tarbell Papers, Allegheny College.

"Several Little Stories by or about President Lincoln." *New York Herald*, February 19, 1864, 5.

"Several Little Stories by or about President Lincoln." *New York Post*, February 17, 1864, 1.

Shackford, James Atkins. *David Crockett: The Man and the Legend.* Edited by John B. Shackford. Chapel Hill: University of North Carolina Press, 1956.

Silver, Andrew. *Minstrelsy and Murder: The Crisis of Southern Humor, 1835–1925.* Baton Rouge: Louisiana State University Press, 2006.

Smith, Charles H. *Bill Arp, So Called: A Side Show of the Southern Side of the War.* New York: Metropolitan Record Office, 1866.

Smith, Michael T. "The Beast Unleashed: Benjamin F. Butler and Conceptions of Masculinity in the Civil War North." *New England Quarterly* 79.2 (2006): 248–76.

"*Southern Punch.*" *Illustrated Civil War Newspapers and Magazines,* 1998–2007. lincolnandthecivilwar.com.

Speed, Joshua Fry. *Reminiscences of Abraham Lincoln and Notes of a Visit to California, Two Lectures.* Louisville: Morton, 1884.

Stampp, Kenneth M. "Lincoln and the Secession Crisis." In *Major Problems in the Civil War and Reconstruction,* edited by Michael Perman, 72–80. Boston: Houghton Mifflin, 1998.

Stedman, Jane W. "American English in *Punch,* 1841–1900." *American Speech* 28.3 (1953): 171–80.

Stern, Philip Van Doren. Headnote. "Address at Cooper Institute, New York." In Lincoln, *Life and Writings,* 568–69.

———. Headnote. "From Lincoln's Opening Speech at the Second Joint Debate at Freeport, Illinois." In Lincoln, *Life and Writings,* 474–75.

Stevens, Walter B. *A Reporter's Lincoln.* Edited by Michael Burlingame. Lincoln: University of Nebraska Press 1998.

Stewart, Samuel Boyd. "Joseph Glover Baldwin." PhD diss., Vanderbilt University, 1941.

Stowe, Harriet Beecher. *Men of Our Times, or Leading Patriots of the Day.* 1868. Hartford: Hartford, 1968.

Strange, James F. *Sketches and Eccentricities of Col. David Crockett, of West Tennessee.* New York: Harper, 1833.

Streicher, Lawrence H. "On a Theory of Political Caricature." *Comparative Studies in History* 9 (1967): 427–45.

Strother, David H. [attributed]. Lincoln as monkey. January 14, 1863, Richmond, Virginia. Lilly Library, Indiana University, Bloomington.

Sumner, Charles. *The Promises of the Declaration of Independence: Eulogy on Abraham Lincoln, Delivered before the Municipal Authorities of the City of Boston, June 1, 1865.* Boston: Ticknor and Fields, 1865.

Tandy, Jeannette. *Crackerbox Philosophers in American Humor and Satire.* Port Washington: Columbia University Press, 1925.

Tebbel, John. *The Media in America.* New York: Crowell, 1974.

Tenniel, John. "Britannia Sympathises with Columbia." *Punch* (London), May 6, 1865, 183. Alfred Whital Stern Collection of Lincolniana, Rare Book and Special Collections Division, Library of Congress, Washington, DC.

———. "The Great 'Cannon Game.'" Cartoon. *Punch* (London), May 9, 1863, 191.

Thomas, Benjamin. *"Lincoln's Humor" and Other Essays*. Edited by Michael Burlingame. Urbana: University of Illinois Press, 2002.

Thompson, Todd. "'Invectives . . . against the Americans': Benjamin Franklin's Satiric Nationalism in the Stamp Act Crisis." *Journal of the Midwest Modern Language Association* 40.1 (2007): 25–36.

———. "Representative Nobodies: The Politics of Benjamin Franklin's Satiric Personae, 1722–1757." *Early American Literature* 46.3 (2011): 449–80.

Thompson, W. Fletcher, Jr. *The Image of War: The Pictorial Reporting of the American Civil War*. New York: Yoseloff, 1959.

Trent, W. P. "A Retrospect of American Humor." In *Critical Essays on American Humor*, edited by William Bedford Clark and W. Craig Turner, 32–46. Boston: Hall, 1984.

"The Tribune Offering the Chief Magistracy to the Western Cincinnatus." Cartoon. *Momus*, June 9, 1860, 73.

Uncle Abe's Comic Almanac, 1865. Philadelphia: Fisher, 1864.

"'Uncle Sam' Making New Arrangements." Poster cartoon. New York: Currier and Ives, 1860.

Vinton, Ellen A. "Who Are Our American Humorists?" *Peterson Magazine*, 1895, 1159–64.

Volck, Adalbert Johann. "Lincoln Signing the Emancipation Proclamation." Engraving. October 1862. Lilly Library, Indiana University, Bloomington, Indiana.

Ward, A., Jr. "A. Ward, Jr. on the Presidency." *Father Abraham* (Reading, PA), August 1, 1864, 1.

Weber, Jennifer L. "Lincoln's Critics: The Copperheads." *Journal of the Abraham Lincoln Association* 32.1 (2011): 33–47.

Welles, Gideon. *The Diary of Gideon Welles, Vol. 1*. Boston: Houghton Mifflin, 1911.

West, Richard S. *"Budget of Fun." Illustrated Civil War Newspapers and Magazines*, 1998–2007. lincolnandthecivilwar.com.

———. *"Phunny Phellow." Illustrated Civil War Newspapers and Magazines*, 1998–2007. lincolnandthecivilwar.com.

Whipple, Wayne. *The Story-Life of Lincoln: A Biography Composed of Five Hundred True Stories*. Philadelphia: Winston, 1908.

Whitman, Walt. "Walt Whitman to Nathaniel Bloom and John F. S. Gray. March 19–20, 1863." In *The Correspondence*, edited by Edwin Haviland Miller, 1:1842–67, 80–85. New York: New York University Press, 1961.

Bibliography

Wilson, Douglas L. *Lincoln before Washington: New Perspectives on the Illinois Years.* Urbana: University of Illinois Press, 1997.

———. *Lincoln's Sword: The Presidency and the Power of Words.* New York: Knopf, 2006.

Wilson, Douglas L., and Rodney O. Davis, eds. *Herndon's Informants.* Chicago: University of Illinois Press, 1998.

Wilson, Rufus Rockwell. *Lincoln in Caricature.* New York: Horizon, 1953.

Winkle, Kenneth J. *The Young Eagle: The Rise of Abraham Lincoln.* Dallas: Taylor, 2001.

Winter, Aaron McLean. "The Laughing Doves of 1812 and the Satiric Endowment of Antiwar Rhetoric in the United States." *PMLA* 124.5 (2009): 1562–81.

"With All Thy Faults." Cartoon. *Phunny Phellow,* January 1865, 8–9.

Winship, Michael. "Manufacturing and Book Production." In Casper, Groves, Nissenbaum, and Winship, *History of the Book,* 40–69.

Woodford, Frank B. *Lewis Cass: The Last Jeffersonian.* New Brunswick: Rutgers University Press, 1950.

Woods, Michael. "Lincoln's Health Draws Scrutiny." *Pittsburgh (PA) Post-Gazette,* July 25, 2000, 25.

A Workingman's Reasons for the Re-Election of Abraham Lincoln. 1864. Pamphlet. Lilly Library, Indiana University, Bloomington, Indiana.

Wyllie, Irvin G. *The Self-Made Man in America: The Myth of Rags to Riches.* New Brunswick: Rutgers University Press, 1954.

"Yankee Humor." *Every Saturday: A Journal of Choice Reading,* March 16, 1867.

Ye Book of Copperheads. Philadelphia: Leypoldt, 1863.

Zall, P. M., ed. *Abe Lincoln Laughing: Humorous Anecdotes from Original Sources by and about Abraham Lincoln.* Berkeley: University of California Press, 1982.

———. *Abe Lincoln's Legacy of Laughter: Humorous Stories by and about Abraham Lincoln.* Knoxville: University of Tennessee Press, 2007.

———. *Lincoln on Lincoln.* Lexington: University Press of Kentucky, 1999.

Index

Italicized page numbers indicate figures.

"Abduction of the Yankee Goddess of Liberty," 90, 92, *92*
abolition, 30, 77–78, *78*, 99–100. *See also* Emancipation Proclamation; slavery
Abraham Africanus I (Feeks), 28–29, 93, 95, 104, 105
Abraham Lincoln, the Young Backwoods Boy (Alger), 88
"Abraham Lincoln. Foully Assassinated, April 14, 1865," 113, 154n42
Aesop's fables, 9, 12–13, 24, 29, 145n6, 145n8
Alger, Horatio, 65; *Abraham Lincoln, the Young Backwoods Boy*, 88
American War, The (Morgan), 112–13
Aristotle, 44, 45, 148n8. *See also* irony
Arp, Bill (Charles H. Smith), 29, 96, 98–100, 103–4; *Bill Arp, So Called: A Side Show of the Southern Side of the War*, 29, 104

Baldwin, Joseph Glover, 9, 19; *Flush Times in Alabama and Mississippi*, 17–18

Baker, Joseph E.: "Columbia Demands Her Children!," 25, *27*; "Rail Splitter at Work Repairing the Union," 79–80, *80*
Bakhtin, Mikhail, 144nn16–17
Bank of Illinois. *See* Illinois state bank
Beecher, Henry Ward, 83
Bell, John, 77, *77*, 127, *127*
Bellew, Frank, 1, 34; "Good Uncle and the Naughty Boy,"131, *132*; "Lincoln's Last Warning," 77, *78*; "Long Abraham a Little Longer," 133, *134*; "National Joker," 1, 25, *27*, 28, 31, *32*; "Presidential Cobblers and Wire-Pullers," 130, *131*; "'Rail' Old Western Gentleman," 123; "This Reminds Me of a Little Joke," 31–32, *32*, 131–32
Benedict, Almon H., 125
Bible, 12, 14, 19, 43
Biglow Papers, The (Lowell), 2, 23
Black Hawk War, 5, 49–52
black Republican, 94–102, *97*, *103*. *See also* Republican Party
"'Boy' Lost!," 125–26, *126*. *See also* Douglas, Stephen A. (Senator)

Brady, Mathew, 119, 155n9
Bray, Robert, 8, 14, 43, 44, 61, 71, 145n6, 145n8, 146n19, 148n52
Breckinridge, John C., 76, 77, 77, 127, 127
"Britannia Sympathises with Columbia" (Tenniel), 113
Brooks, Noah, 9, 24, 38, 60–61, 121
Browne, Charles Farrar (Artemus Ward), 1, 9, 23, 24, 98, 139
Buchanan, James (President), 16, 76
Bunker, Gary L., 8, 109, 154n3, 156n29, 156n33
Burke, Kenneth, 5
Burns, Robert, 12,
Butler, Benjamin (General), 99–100

caricature, 1–2, 24, 73–74, 81, 114, 116, 118, 119, 121–23, 124, 128–29, 130, 133, 136–39. See also political cartoons
Carpenter, Francis, 18, 115
Cass, Lewis (Senator, General), 5, 49–55, 57, 149n18
Chase, Salmon P. (Secretary of Treasury), 31, 62–63, 93
Cincinnatus, 74–75, 75, 78–79, 123
Civil War, 12–13, 14–15, 24–25, 27, 28, 29, 30, 36, 37, 38–39, 61, 77, 86, 87, 89, 101, 102–5, 107, 109, 110, 110, 130, 135; Fort Sumter, 61–63, 150n42
Clay, Henry (Senator), 68
Columbia, 25, 27, 78–79, 79, 109, 111, 113, 133, 135, 135
"Columbia Demands Her Children!" (Baker), 25, 27
Comic News (London), 106–7, 109–12. See also humor periodicals
Congress. See House of Representatives
Conwell, Russell H., 24, 120
"Cooperation," 80–81, 82
Cooper Union speech, 94, 119, 120, 155n13

Copperheads, 12, 13, 87, 89, 90, 94, 96, 104–5, 106, 152n2
Crockett, David (Congressman), 4, 47–48, 50, 69–71, 151nn13–14
Currier and Ives: "Rail Splitter at Work Repairing the Union" (Baker), 79–80, 80; "'Uncle Sam' Making New Arrangements," 76–77, 77

Davis, Jefferson (President of Confederacy), 77–78, 78, 107, 107–8, 131, 132, 133, 135, 136
Democratic Campaign Songster, The, 117–18
Democratic Party, 4, 14, 22, 50, 52–53, 55, 56, 58, 75–76, 89, 105, 125, 152n2
Douglas, Stephen A. (Senator), 14, 16–17, 55, 56–61, 70, 76, 77, 77, 94, 105, 118, 120, 122, 123–28, 126, 127, 128, 130, 131, 156n29. See also Kansas-Nebraska Act
Downing, Jack (Seba Smith), 15, 145–46n14
Dred Scott ruling, 59

Edwards, Ninian W., 47, 57
Emancipation Proclamation, 77–78, 78, 90, 91, 92, 93, 98–100, 102, 103, 135, 137
Emerson, Ralph Waldo, 10

Father Abraham, 139
Feeks, J. F., 29, 100, 104–5; Abraham Africanus I, 28–29, 93, 95, 104, 105; Lincoln Catechism, 29, 51, 93, 94, 100–102, 104–5; Lincolniana, or Humors of Uncle Abe, 29, 33, 33, 96, 97, 104–5
Flush Times in Alabama and Mississippi (Baldwin), 17–18
Fort Sumter, 61–63, 150n42
Ford, Thomas (Governor), 42–43
Forquer, George, 45–46, 70

Frank Leslie's Budget of Fun, 25, 26, 30, 74, 78, 79, 113–14, 131, *132*, 135, 137, *137*, *138*. *See also* humor periodicals

Frank Leslie's Illustrated Newspaper, 9–10, 12, 17, 72, 80, *81*, 84, *84*, 133, *136*

Franklin, Benjamin, 4, 21, 42, 65

Fun (London), 109, 110, 112. *See also* humor periodicals

Funniest of Phun, 25, *27*, 28, 74. *See also* humor periodicals

Georgia Scenes (Longstreet), 19, 56

God Bless Abraham Lincoln: A Solemn Discourse by a Local Preacher, 99–100, 102

"Good Gracious, Abraham Lincoln!," 78–79, *79*, 133

"Good Uncle and the Naughty Boy, The" (Bellew), 131, *132*

Grant, Ulysses S. (General), 15, 23–24, 135, *137*

"Great and Astonishing Trick of Old Abe, the Western Juggler," 25, *26*

"Great 'Cannon Game,' The," (Tenniel), *107*, 107–8

Greeley, Horace, 74–75, *75*

Halpine, Charles Graham (Miles O'Reilly), 36–38

Harper's magazines, 9, 16, 17, *32*, 56, 72, 77, 78, 119, 130, 131, 133, *134*

Harris, George Washington (Sut Lovingood), 18–19, 96, 97–98, 104; *Sut Lovingood: Yarns Spun by a Nat'ral Born Durn'd Fool*, 18–19

Harris, Joel Chandler, 2, 3, 7

Harrison, William Henry (President), 66, 69

Hay, John, 36–38

Herndon, William, 10, 18, 39, 43, 46, 49

Holzer, Harold, 8, 74, 121, 153nn23–24, 154n42, 154n3, 156n20

"Honest Old Abe and the Little Boy in Search of His Mother—A Sensation Story," 124–25

Hooper, Johnson (Simon Suggs), 19

House Divided speech, 14, 58

House of Representatives, 5, 16, 33, 47–48, 49, 53, 54, 68, 69, 71, 99, 101. *See also* Lincoln, Abraham: congressman

Howard, J. H., 25, *28*

Howells, William Dean, 67–68, 70

humor periodicals, 1, 25, 28–30, 74, 89, 106–7, 110–14, 124, 154n30. *See also specific periodical titles*

"I Knew Him, Horatio" (Howard), 25, *28*

Illinois state bank, 21–22, 44

Illinois State Register, 48–49

illustrated news, 71–73, 74, 85, 118, 119. *See also specific periodical titles*

"In for His Second Innings" (Morgan), 109–10, *112*

irony, 5, 11, 44, 45, 50, 59, 99, 143n8, 148n8. *See also* satire theory

Jackson, Andrew (President, General), 52, 66, 69, 118

"Jeff Davis's November Nightmare," 133–34, *136*

"Job for the New Cabinet Maker, A," 80, *81*

Joe Miller's Jests, 9, 14, 23, 24, 28.

joke books, 1, 9, 14, 30–31, 32–34, *33*, *34*, 35, 96, 97, 108–9

Johnson, Andrew (Vice President), 79–80, *80*

Kansas-Nebraska Act, 14, 16, 58, 59, 95, 124–25. *See also* Douglas, Stephen A. (Senator)

Kerr, Orpheus C. (R. H. Newell), 1, 23; *Palace Beautiful and Other Poems*, 23–24

"Last Rail Split by 'Honest Old Abe,'
The," 75–76, *76*
Life of Abraham Lincoln, The (Howells),
67–68, 70
Lincoln, Abraham: appearance, 64, 73,
78, 94, 96–98, 102, 106, 108, 113,
115–39, *117, 127, 128, 129, 131, 132,
134, 135, 136, 137, 138,* 155n9, 155n12;
campaign biography (1860), 41–42,
51–52, 67, 74, 120, 150n8; childhood,
41, 43, 66, 67, 68; congressman, 5,
42, 49–55, 56, 68, 71; Cooper Union
speech, 94, 119, 120, 155n13; education, 39, 41–42; Emancipation Proclamation, 77–78, *78,* 90, 91, 92, 93,
98–100, 102, *103,* 135, *137;* House Divided speech, 14, 58; lawyer, 15, 19,
21, 41, 67–68, 115; Lincoln-Douglas
Debates, 16–17, 56, 58–61, 94, 120,
123–24 (*see also* Douglas, Stephen
A. [Senator]); New England speaking tour, 54–55; newspaper satires,
21–23, 38–39; "rail-splitter" image,
30, 66–69, 73, 74–80, *75, 76, 77, 78,
79, 80,* 82, 85, 88, 93, 106, 113, 123,
124, 128, *128,* 130; "President's Last,
Shortest, and Best Speech," 38–39;
"Rebecca" letter, 21–23, 47; stories,
3, 6, 7, 9–20, *13,* 25, *27,* 28–31, *32,*
32–38, 48, 60, 63, 64, 85, 93, 96, 115,
116, 119, 131–32
"Lincoln, Douglas, and the Rail-Fence
Handicap," 128, *128*
Lincoln Catechism, The (Feeks), 29, 51,
93, 94, 100–102, 104–5
Lincolniana, or Humors of Uncle Abe
(Feeks), 29, 33, *33,* 96, *97,* 104–5
"Lincoln Signing the Emancipation
Proclamation" (Volck), 90, *91*
"Lincoln's Last Warning" (Bellew), 77, *78*
Linder, Usher F., 44–45, *46,* 47, 70
lithography, 71, 72, 103–4, 151n18
Locke, David R. (Petroleum V. Nasby)
9, 23, 24

"Log Cabin Built by President Lincoln
in Kentucky," 84, *84*
"Long Abraham a Little Longer"
(Bellew), 133, *134*
Longstreet, Augustus, 19, 56
Lovingood, Sut (George Washington
Harris), 18–19, 96, 97–98, 104; *Sut
Lovingood: Yarns Spun by a Nat'ral
Born Durn'd Fool,* 18–19
Lowell, James Russell, 83, 108–9; *Bi-
glow Papers,* 2, 23

"Masks and Faces," 90, *91,* 110
Matheny, James H., 23, 46
"May the Best Man Win" (Nast), 129,
129, 131, 132
McClellan, George B. (General), 25, *28,*
31, *32,* 109, *110,* 129, *129,* 130–32,
132
Mexican War. *See* U.S.-Mexico War
Momus, 74–76, *75, 76. See also* humor
periodicals
Morgan, Matt, 109–110, 112–13; *Amer-
ican War,* 112–13; "In for His Second
Innings," 109–10, *112;* "Pull Devil—
Pull Baker," 109, *110;* "Vampire,"
109, *111*

Nasby, Petroleum V. (David R. Locke),
9, 23, 24
Nashville (TN) Union and American,
96–98, 104
Nast, Thomas, 153n24; "May the Best
Man Win," 129, *129,* 131, 132; "Presi-
dent Lincoln's Inaugural," 86–87, *87*
"National Joker, The" (Bellew), 1, 25,
27, 28, 31, *32*
Newell, R. H. (Orpheus C. Kerr), 1, 23;
Palace Beautiful and Other Poems,
23–24
Newman, William: "Phenomenon of
Portraiture," 136–37, *138;* "Tallest
Ruler on the Globe," 135–36, *137*
New York Herald, 34–35, 36–38

New York Illustrated News, 72, 86–87, 87, 130, 131
New York Post, 34–35, 36
New York Times, 10, 111–12, 154n42
New York Tribune. *See* Greeley, Horace
New York World, 25
Noland, F. M. (Pete Whetstone), 21
North American Review, 88–89
Norton, Charles Eliot, 86, 88–89

Old Abe's Joker, or Wit at the White House, 33–34, *34*, 35
Old Abe's Jokes, Fresh from Abraham's Bosom, 30–31, 33–34, 108, 147n44. *See also* joke books
Only Authentic Life of Abraham Lincoln, The, 50–51, 116–17, *117*, 120
O'Reilly, Miles (Charles Graham Halpine), 36–38

Palace Beautiful and Other Poems (Kerr), 23–24
"Phenomenon of Portraiture, A" (Newman), 136–37, *138*
photography, 72, 118, 119, 121, 155n9
Phunny Phellow, 74, 124, 129, 133, *135*. *See also* humor periodicals
physical labor, 41, 66–68, 71, 73–83, 113, 114, 118, 123, 128
Pierce, Franklin (President), 55–56, 122–23, 156n21
political cartoons, 1, 8, 28, 32, 72–74, 80, 81, 109, 121–24, 127, 130, 133, 147n46, 154n3, 156n20. *See also* caricature
"Political Race, A," 127, *127*
popular sovereignty. *See* Kansas-Nebraska Act
"Presidential Cobblers and Wire-Pullers" (Bellew), 130, *131*
"President Lincoln's Inaugural" (Nast), 86–87, *87*
"Pull Devil—Pull Baker" (Morgan), 109, *110*

Punch (London), 106, *107*, 107–8, 110–12, 113–14, 154n30. *See also* humor periodicals

"'Rail' Old Western Gentleman, A" (Bellew), 123
"Rail Splitter at Work Repairing the Union, The" (Baker), 79–80, *80*
Republican Party, 58–59, 62, 64, 66, 75, 89, 90, 94–96, 102, 105, 150n8, 152n2

Sangamo Journal, 21, 22, 23
satanic imagery, 90–94, *91*, *92*, 100, 105, 109–10, *110*
satire theory, 2–7, 11, 19, 24, 44, 50, 61, 73, 143n8, 144n12, 144nn16–17
satirist-satirized, 4, 5, 44, 139
satirist-statesmen, 4, 5, 35, 144n9
Scott, Winfield (General), 55, 122
Scribner's Monthly, 60–61
secession, 25, 30, 62–63, 86–87, 92, 150n42
self-made man, 7, 42, 49, 52, 60, 64–70, 71, 73, 74, 83–85, 87–89, 90, 93, 105, 106, 108–9, 130, 150n3, 150n8
Seward, William (Secretary of State), 10, 29
Shakespeare, William, 12, 25
Shields, James (Senator, Brigadier General), 14–15, 22, 45
slavery, 2, 16, 18, 38–39, 77–78, *78*, 90, 94, 99, 101, 102, 148n55. *See also* abolition
Smith, Charles H. (Bill Arp), 29, 96, 98–100, 103–4; *Bill Arp, So Called: A Side Show of the Southern Side of the War*, 29, 104
Smith, Seba (Jack Downing), 15, 145–46n14
Southern Confederacy, 29, 98, 104
Southern Illustrated News, 90, 91, 110, 152n7

Southern Punch, 29, 92, 92. *See also* humor periodicals

southwestern humor, 6, 9, 17–21, 23, 29, 56, 96–99, 104, 106. *See also specific authors and titles*

Speed, Joshua, 12–13, 46

sporting metaphors, 127, 156n29

Stanton, Edwin (Secretary of War), 1, 15

Stowe, Harriet Beecher, 83, 98–100

Suggs, Simon (Johnson Hooper), 19

Sut Lovingood: Yarns Spun by a Nat'ral Born Durn'd Fool (Lovingood), 18–19

"Tallest Ruler on the Globe, The" (Newman), 135–36, *137*

tariffs, 15–16

Taylor, E. D. (Colonel), 46–47

Taylor, Zachary (President, General), 50, 52, 66

Tenniel, John, 154n42; "Britannia Sympathises with Columbia," 113; "Great 'Cannon Game,'" *107*, 107–8

"This Reminds Me of a Little Joke" (Bellew), 31–32, *32*, 131–32

Thomas, Jesse B., 49

Todd, Mary (Mrs. Abraham Lincoln), 22, 29, 119

"Tribune Offering the Chief Magistracy to the Western Cincinnatus, The," 74–75, *75*

Uncle Abe's Comic Almanac, 35

Uncle Sam, 76–77, *77*, 108, 129, *129*, 131, 152n26

"'Uncle Sam' Making New Arrangements," 76–77, *77*

U.S.-Mexico War, 2, 49–50, 55, 156n21

"Vampire, The" (Morgan), 109, *111*

Van Buren, Martin (President), 54

Vanity Fair, 74, 80–81, *82*. *See also* humor periodicals

Volck, Adalbert Johann, 102, 153n24; "Lincoln Signing the Emancipation Proclamation," 90, *91*

Ward, Artemus (Charles Farrar Browne), 1, 9, 23, 24, 98, 139

Washington, D.C., Daily Chronicle, 38–39

Whetstone, Pete (F. M. Noland), 21

Whig Party, 16, 20, 21, 22, 23, 46, 47, 52, 53, 54–55, 68–71, 146n29

Whitman, Walt, 115, 118

"*Wide Awake*" Poem, A (Benedict), 125

"With All Thy Faults," 133, *135*

Ye Book of Copperheads, 12, *13*

Zall, P. M., 6, 8, 13, 32, 71, 115, 147n44

Todd Nathan Thompson is an associate professor of English at Indiana University of Pennsylvania, where he also serves as coordinator for the master's in literature and the master's in composition and literature programs. His work has appeared in *ESQ: A Journal of the American Renaissance*, *Early American Literature*, *Nineteenth-Century Prose*, *Scholarly Editing*, *Studies in American Humor*, and elsewhere.